The ARMOR OF GOD

PRISCILLA SHIRER

Lifeway Press®
Nashville, Tennessee

© 2018 Priscilla Shirer
Reprinted Nov. 2018, May 2019, July 2019, Sept. 2019, Mar. 2020,
June 2020, Sept. 2020, Jan. 2021, June 2021, Dec. 2021, Oct. 2022

ISBN 9781535924191
Item 005806985

Dewey decimal classification: 248.83
Subject headings: RELIGION/CHRISTIAN MINISTRY/YOUTH

To order additional copies of this resource, write to Lifeway Church
Resources Customer Service; 200 Powell Place, Suite 100, Brentwood,
TN 37027; fax 615.251.5933; phone toll free 800.458.2772; email
orderentry@lifeway.com; order online at www.lifeway.com.

Cover art Alexis Ward, The Visual Republic

Printed in the United States of America.

Student Ministry Publishing
Lifeway Christian Resources
200 Powell Place, Suite 100
Brentwood, TN 37027

TABLE OF CONTENTS

PRISCILLA SHIRER

is a homemade cinnamon roll baker, Bible teacher and bestselling author who didn't know she was on *The New York Times*' list (*Fervent*) until somebody else told her. Because who has time to check lists when you are raising three sons. When Priscilla and Jerry (who have been married for 19 years) are not busy leading *Going Beyond Ministries*, they spend most of their time cleaning up after and trying to satisfy the appetites of their very large boys.

Priscilla has written many Bible studies on a myriad of different biblical topics and personalities including *Discerning the Voice of God, Gideon, and Jonah*. She first wrote *The Armor of God* Bible study in 2015 and now she is excited to share this updated and adapted version with you.

INTRODUCTION

Just so you know what you're getting into …

This study should be unique. A bit different from others you've done. Because, by the time you've finished reading (and working) through it, the front cover shouldn't be able to close neatly back over on itself. It should be noticeably disfigured from heartfelt use. War-torn. An impossible option for regifting at Christmas time.

Pages should be ripped out (literally) and written on. The edges tattered and the corners curled. I want your mom afraid to touch it without using plastic gloves. Perhaps even the salad tongs. Unmistakable signs that you've been here, and been involved here, invested here.

Think of this workbook as industrial-grade survival gear. Duct tape and super glue. Leather straps lashed around it. Old shoelaces maybe. In tight double knots. Whatever it takes to keep it all together.

Because this is war. The fight of your life. A very real enemy has been strategizing and scheming against you, assaulting you, coming after your emotions, your mind, your future. In fact, he's doing it right this second. Right where you're sitting. Right where you are.

But I say his reign of terror stops here. Stops now. He might keep coming, but he won't have victory anymore. Because, starting today, we will be armed and dangerous. Prepared to stand firm against his insidious schemes.

And, as we learn about what to wear to ensure victory, we're simultaneously going to engage in what to do to guarantee it. Each week, we'll employ the secret weapon that has been divinely authorized by God Himself to stop the devil in his tracks.

We are going to pray.

Not just talk about it. No, we are going to do it.

As we equip ourselves with the armor of God, we are going to close each week by giving you an opportunity to develop a prayer strategy to promptly put the enemy in his place. Strategy? Yes.

Targeted. Specific. Precise. Detailed.

So that the enemy will know beyond any reasonable doubt that his number is up and his game is done.

Whatever you do, please do not ignore this portion of your study. It's not an addendum—a cutesy exercise to take up time. No, it's the essential key to victory. At the back of this book, you'll find some Prayer Strategies (page 192) and some perforated pages purposefully designed for you to craft your prayers. Pull them out of this book, and then post them in a place where you'll see them often and pray them with passion regularly. Out loud. Where the devil can hear you clearly and know that you aren't messing around.

I invite you to fully engage in every minute of this study. Don't allow the enemy one more day of victory in your life. His reign of terror stops today.

And it stops with me and you—students equipped with the armor of God.

Victoriously,

Priscilla Shirer

EPHESIANS 6:10-19

10 Finally, be strong in the Lord and in the strength of His might.

11 Put on the full armor of God, so that you will be able to stand firm against the schemes of the devil.

12 For our struggle is not against flesh and blood, but against the rulers, against the powers, against the world forces of this darkness, against the spiritual forces of wickedness in the heavenly places.

13 Therefore, take up the full armor of God, so that you will be able to resist in the evil day, and having done everything, to stand firm.

14 Stand firm therefore, having girded your loins with truth, and having put on the breastplate of righteousness,

15 and having shod your feet with the preparation of the gospel of peace;

16 in addition to all, taking up the shield of faith with which you will be able to extinguish all the flaming arrows of the evil one.

17 And take the helmet of salvation, and the sword of the Spirit, which is the word of God.

18 With all prayer and petition pray at all times in the Spirit, and with this in view, be on the alert with all perseverance and petition for all the saints,

19 and pray…

SIZING UP THE ENEMY

Think about your attitude toward prayer. Would you say prayer is powerful? Why or why not?

If you answered yes, in what ways do your life and actions prove that you believe prayer is a powerful weapon?

My cousin Jonathan works across the street from a clinic where abortions are offered. Once a week, he and a few of his friends stand near the clinic parking lot—200 meters or so away so it's not considered trespassing—and look for opportunities to talk about the value of life with the people who come to this clinic.

Last winter, Jonathan and his friends were outside the clinic on a cold Friday—and they didn't really want to be there. It was 20 degrees, so of course they didn't want to be there! It was cold, a bit rainy, but Jonathan had made a commitment, so he showed up.

No one stopped. No one wanted to talk with them. That day in the cold weather, as he was feeling exhausted and wondering why he was even there, Jonathan told me that he was pretty upset with God. He actually asked the Lord, "Why am I here again?"

Then a truck pulled in. Jonathan could tell that a teen girl was in the passenger's seat, maybe 17-20 years old. An older white-haired gentleman was driving, perhaps her father or grandfather. The man parked the truck, but no one got out. Jonathan could tell the passengers were talking. He could see them turn their faces toward each other, watched the girl bury her head in her hands and cry. Still, they sat in the car. Jonathan realized that in this moment, everything hung in the balance.

He also realized that he wasn't useless, that he had a powerful weapon in his arsenal even as he stood a distance away. War was being waged in that car, and Jonathan could pray and swing the balance of this girl's decision.

After about 15 minutes of the passengers talking and Jonathan praying, the truck drove away. In that moment, on that day, a child's life had been spared. Jonathan never got the opportunity to talk to the young woman, but he had played a powerful role in her battle.

Jonathan believed that he had a powerful tool to wield in an invisible battle being waged in the heavenly places. How can you see evidence of that war being waged in your life? In your community? In the world?

There is an invisible battle taking place around us—and you and I get the privilege of swaying the balance toward life in the name of Jesus Christ! You and I have the opportunity to suit up, put on some armor that works, go to battle, and see victory declared in our lives and in the lives of the people we love. Over the next six weeks, we will look at Paul's Letter to the Ephesians in a new light and really see and understand that God has given us the tools to influence and make a difference in the things we are facing in this life. Every day.

Read Ephesians 6:10-19. These verses may feel familiar to you. Even so, what words or phrases stand out? What did you notice that you hadn't before?

How many pieces of armor are listed in this passage of Scripture?

Underline each piece of armor listed in the passage, then circle every mention of the word "pray" or "prayer."

Prayer makes a difference. In other words, there aren't just six pieces of armor like we've thought for so long. There are seven because without prayer, the others aren't activated. They're not infused. They're not plugged in so that we can tap into all the power the armor is supposed to bring into our lives.

So we're not just going to talk about six pieces of armor over the next six weeks. We've got a seventh, and it's going to permeate every single thing we do throughout these weeks of Bible study together.

Focus in on verse 12. Read it aloud several times, carefully considering each phrase and what it reveals.

This makes it very clear that there *is* a battle. The devil wants us to think there isn't, but there is. And it's *unavoidable*. Your relationship with Jesus marks you as Satan's enemy, and he will wage war against you. The choice is not whether open war is upon us, but whether we will engage the enemy or not, whether we will experience the victory Christ has won for us on Calvary.

1. The battle is _____.

Satan is real, but he wants you to think he's not. Because he is *invisible*, we can't physically see, taste, touch, or hear every weapon he will use against us. But understand this: Satan is not God's peer or counterpart. He has limitations and boundaries.

2. The enemy is _____.

Identify the qualities we know only God possesses. Use the listed Scripture passages to help you place the following answers in the correct space. *(work miracles; omnipresent; eternal; omniscient)*

Only our God is _____. (Ps. 139:7-10; Isa. 43:1-4, Col. 1:17)

Only our God is _____. (Job 37:14-17; Isa. 40:28; Isa. 55:8-9)

Only our God can _____. (Deut. 10:21; Job 5:8-9; Acts 19:11-12)

Only our God is _____. (Ex. 3:13-15; Ps. 90:1-4; Rev. 1:7-8)

We have no reason to be afraid because if the omniscient, omnipresent, eternal, all-powerful God is for you, then it doesn't matter who or what is against you. We don't have to be afraid, but we do need to be on guard.

Underline the final phrase of verse 12, "in the heavenly places." Then, jot down a few notes about heavenly places revealed elsewhere in the Book of Ephesians.

• **Ephesians 1:3** _____

• **Ephesians 1:20** _____

• **Ephesians 3:10** _____

• **Ephesians 2:5-6** _____

This tells us that even though the battle is unavoidable and the enemy is invisible, the location is *accessible*. Because we have a relationship with Jesus Christ, we are seated with Him in heavenly places. We have full rights and privileges to access the heavenly places where all the blessings and tools we need to combat the enemy are stored.

3. The location is _____.

God has given us a divinely mandated and approved mechanism to access the power we have available to us in the heavenly realm. What do you think it is?

We are able to access all the spiritual resources, divine authority, and blessings we have been given to stand against the enemy. If you refuse to pray and take it seriously, you're wasting your time trying to stand firm against the enemy. Prayer activates the armor. So pray consistently and fervently.

Next, I want you to read Isaiah 59:17-18 and 2 Corinthians 10:3-4. What do these verses teach us about the armor and the weapons God has given us?

It's literally God's armor that He is taking off and handing to you—not some second-hand thrift store armor or cheap imitation of the real thing. Only the best weapons will do, and they are not *physical*. It is the very same armor God put on in Isaiah 59.

4. Your weapons are not _____.

How do these weapons bring real change rather than temporary solutions?

Never, ever forget this final truth.

In Jesus' life, death, and resurrection, the victory has already been won on your behalf, and that victory is *irrevocable*. Scripture tells us that the enemy does not stand a chance. He knows his time is running out. Revelation assures us that victory will ultimately come, and we will experience it.

5. The victory is _____.

But we don't have to wait. Put on the armor of God and experience that victory today!

DAY 1

WRESTLING MATCH

I first began writing Bible studies more than ten years ago. At the time, my sons were very young. Jackson, my oldest, was two; Jerry Jr., my second, was three months old; and our youngest, Jude—that boy wasn't even a thought in our minds yet.

Since then, however, my babies have turned gargantuan. As they've grown older and stronger, they've also begun to realize their strength. So wrestling has become not only one of their favorite sports to watch, but also to undertake. With each other and, sadly, with me.

Sometimes one of them will spring from around a corner, nestle a shoulder into my waistline, and sling me, flailing and begging, over his shoulder. His brothers will laugh hysterically while I'm hauled to the sofa, tossed onto the cushions, and then forcibly pinned down, no hope of escape. Glad it's funny ... to them.

There's nothing like writing out Scripture to imprint it on your heart and encourage you to let it change your actions. We'll be doing it a lot throughout our study. So turn to Ephesians 6:12 in your Bible or on page 7 of your book. Write the verse in the space provided below.

Reading back over what you've written, circle what the Bible says you are *not* wrestling against, then underline the four entities that you *are* wrestling against.

No matter which translation you copied, one word is similar in most: *wrestle*. Some translate it as *struggle*. The original wording that the apostle Paul used here—*palē* (pronounced PAL-ay)—denotes a contest or fight between opponents, waged in close, hand-to-hand combat with the goal of pinning down and defeating one's rival.

In the oval below, write the name of the most difficult person, most stressful problem, or the thing in your life that feels the most overwhelming right now. Mention several issues if you'd like. Take your time. You'll be referring back to this list throughout your study.

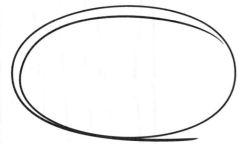

In what ways are you currently "wrestling" with this person or circumstance?

Whatever you've written above—whoever or whatever it is—it is not your real problem. Hear that again: IT is NOT your REAL problem. The most troubling things in your life—things you comprehend with your five physical senses—are not your real issues. Though you may be wrestling with them verbally, emotionally, financially, even physically, you are wasting precious time and energy that needs to be reserved for the real culprit—the one who is behind the scenes, striving to direct the details of your difficulties. Everything that occurs in the visible, physical world is directly connected to the wrestling match being waged in the invisible, spiritual world.

Underline the last sentence of the previous paragraph. Then rewrite it in your own words.

Go back to the oval and write "Not the Real Enemy" on the blank beside it.

Your real enemy—the devil—wants you to ignore the spiritual reality behind the physical one. Because as long as you're focused on what you can see with your physical eyes, he can continue to run rampant underneath the surface. The more you disregard him, the more damage he can do. The enemy may be invisible, but he is not fictional. He is very real, and very persistent, waging war against us constantly.

> **THE ENEMY MAY BE INVISIBLE BUT HE IS NOT FICTIONAL.**
> *#ArmorOfGodStudy*

The effects of the war going on in the unseen world reveal themselves in our strained, damaged relationships, emotional instability, mental fatigue, and physical exhaustion. Many of us feel "pinned down" by anger, unforgiveness, pride, comparisons, insecurity, discord, fear … the list goes on and on. But the overarching, primary nemesis behind all these outcomes is the devil himself.

List some of the specific ways you've felt "pinned down" in your life recently. (Use the space in the margin if you need more room.)

relationships

mental

emotional

physical

other

At some point during my wrestling matches with the boys, when I've been thoroughly subdued despite my best efforts at fighting back, their father will appear, ready to save and rescue me. The sight of his looming, six-foot-three-inch frame will send all the younger Shirer men careening in a million different directions. All of a sudden, I'm free and back on my feet. Not because I'm particularly strong—in fact, I'm not as strong as my boys are becoming—but because I'm in relationship with someone who is.

Be strong in the Lord and in the strength of His might (Eph. 6:10).

Being a believer doesn't mean you're immune from the assaults of the enemy, but it does give you access to the power of the Father—His power to defend you as well as reverse what's been done to you. If you want to win the fight, the key is realizing you have a direct connection to more spiritual power than is coming against you.

EYE-OPENING

Many scholars agree that Paul's letter to the Ephesians is the gem of his New Testament writings. He wrote it not only to draw attention to the spiritual battle that exists in the invisible, unseen realm, but to also help every believer—those who are in a relationship with God through Jesus—recognize the power they have available to them because of that relationship. For our purposes, we're going to be focusing primarily on the last part of Ephesians. But we'll look at the first half, too, because it helps us to recognize the dynamic spiritual blessings that enable us to accurately apply the commands Paul spelled out in the back half.

Throughout our study, we are going to keep returning to one of the most important yet overlooked aspects of our spiritual armor: prayer. Paul deemed prayer so critical to his explanation of how to gain victory over Satan's power that, as one scholar observed, "Ephesians has proportionately more than 55% as many verses directly related to prayer" as Romans, Paul's longest letter.[1] He even burst right out praying several times while he was writing, as we'll see. And when Paul prays ... man, is he strategic, being sure to tell his readers exactly what he is praying for. He knew prayer was able to change the trajectory of their whole lives. Victory in spiritual warfare is inseparable from prayer.

Read Ephesians 1:18-21 and 3:14-19, and record as many details as you can about the intention of Paul's prayers.

Please notice: Paul wasn't asking in prayer that the Ephesian believers would receive their abundant inheritance of spiritual riches, blessings, power, and authority, but that they would realize it was already theirs. As Christians, they already possessed these things, just as we do. But until they realized it, what good could it accomplish? What benefit would all of God's gifts be to them if they weren't aware they'd been given everything needed to send the enemy running for cover?

In reality, the spiritual armor in Ephesians 6 is merely a repeat—a different way of describing what Paul had already been explaining to them in the first portion of the letter. How could they "put on" or "take up" things they didn't know they had? The first step for them—the first step for us—in using the spiritual resources we've already been given is to ask God to open our spiritual eyes so we can see them.

VISION

The story of Elisha and his vision-impaired servant in 2 Kings 6 is one of my absolute favorite stories in the Bible. The setting is a battle about to ensue between the enraged king of Aram and the nation of Israel.

> **THE FIRST STEP IN PUTTING MY SPIRITUAL RESOURCES TO WORK IS RECOGNIZING THEM.**
> *#ArmorOfGodStudy*

Let's look at it together.

Open your Bible to 2 Kings 6:15-17 and answer the following questions:

1. **What did Elisha's servant see when he woke up (v. 15)?**

2. **Given his next action (vv. 15b-16a), how would you describe the servant's emotional state at that moment?**

3. **What was Elisha's reaction (v. 16)?**

4. **How is Elisha's prayer for his servant (v. 17) similar to Paul's prayer for the Ephesians (Eph. 1:18)?**

Elisha's servant got an eyeful. At first, the only thing he could see was the enemy, which likely left him no other response than fear and anxiety. But then he learned a game-changing spiritual reality: more power was at his disposal and working on his behalf than he could have ever imagined. What his physical eyes could see was no match for what they couldn't see. Elisha's prayer helped make him aware of all the resources and strength on his side fighting against the enemy.

To be confident and victorious, you've got to be able to "see" it.

Take inventory of some of the riches given to you in Christ with which you can pin down the enemy. Write key words from each verse below. When you've completed the list, read it out loud.

- **Ephesians 1:3**

- **Ephesians 1:7-8**

- **Ephesians 1:13**

- **Ephesians 1:18-19**

Hit pause for a minute. Think about those gifts—then realize that these are only the gifts Paul accentuated in one chapter. There are many, many more, and each one connects specifically with your spiritual armor and weapons. But the first key to understanding how they all fit into your ability to pin down the enemy is vision. You cannot use these gifts if you're not able to fully recognize them, if you're not aware that they're available to you, or don't understand how important they are in successfully waging war against the enemy of this world and your soul.

Victory starts here. It starts today. It starts with this: a prayer for vision. So join Paul in asking the Lord to open your eyes more fully throughout these next six weeks so you can not only detect the enemy's activity, but can also become fully aware of the tools God has given you to disarm and defeat him in your life.

Actionable Intel...

Actionable Intel is a phrase often used in a military context to describe the information decoded and gathered about opponents that can be used to secure victory against them in future battles. At the end of each Bible study lesson, I've provided you with an Actionable Intel section to store your most important insights. Use it as a place to collect pieces of spiritual information and debrief from what God has revealed to you through your study. Remember: the intel that God's Spirit is giving you is not just a list of things to know. It's a divine strategy God is giving you to take into the fight. The enemy has been gathering intel to develop a strategy against you. This is your chance to gather information to craft a strategy for victory against him. At the end of each week, you'll use all the intel you've gathered to create a personalized prayer strategy against the enemy.

DAY 2

UNDISGUISED

The first-century Ephesian culture was well acquainted with the spiritual realm. Most everyone who lived in the Mediterranean world during this time period believed evil spirits existed.

So when Paul wrote his letter to the Ephesian church, he would not have had to convince them of their need for countermeasures against demonic influence. They knew they needed it desperately and usually looked to magic to assist. The effects of demonic activity were everywhere.[2]

Today, as we live out our beliefs about the spiritual realm, particularly in relation to Satan, we tend to make one of two mistakes:

1. We overestimate his impact in our lives, living with an inflated, false perspective of his actual influence and abilities. As a result, we give in to undue fear and anxiety.

2. We underestimate him and miscalculate the impact of his influence in our lives. We prioritize what we can see over what we can't. As a result, we discount his influence in our lives and the world.

Which of the above extremes describes most of the people you know?

How does that perspective affect the way those people live? What are some of its more noticeable effects? Explain.

What about you? What's your tendency? Do you personally overestimate or underestimate the enemy's influence in the circumstances of your life? What effect does this inclination have in your life? Prepare to discuss this with your group.

As we discussed in Day 1, we tend to concentrate primarily on what's visible and physical, instead of zeroing in on the invisible and spiritual. Even if we're aware of the enemy's work, we aren't quite sure how to engage him and defeat him.

The enemy keeps his activity so cleverly hidden that we almost forget his existence. Or, at best, we only recognize his presence in a theoretical, nonthreatening way. We are far less quick to discern his schemes, pinpoint his efforts, and proactively combat them the way other cultures (albeit incorrectly at times) may have done. We've become a culture relatively unaware of the enemy's presence, unaware of his conspiracies to destroy our lives, unaware that he's distracting us from reaching our destinies.

Read 2 Corinthians 11:14 in the margin. How have you found this tactic of the enemy to be true in your own life? Explain.

And no wonder! For Satan disguises himself as an angel of light (2 Cor. 11:14, CSB).

Spiritual victory is directly connected to your ability to "undisguise" the enemy. To uncover him. Unveil or unmask him. That's half the battle. But it's the half your enemy doesn't want you to pay much attention to, because once you do, you automatically begin to threaten his power in your life.

The names of the enemy reveal his character, intention, and activity. See Digging Deeper 1 on page 23 for more insight.

Yesterday, we talked about the importance of having vision and realizing the riches that are made available to us through Christ. One of the most critical roles our vision plays is helping us to detect the enemy lurking behind the surface of some of life's most pressing difficulties. Let's spend more time on that today.

Write down the four entities with which you are truly engaged in battle from Ephesians 6:12.

These evil, supernatural forces are the same principalities and authorities Paul mentioned earlier (Eph. 1:21; 3:10). They operate under the enemy's control and carry out his wicked purposes and schemes. The Bible doesn't give us a ton of details about how the devil's dark forces are organized, but "this list of spiritual powers has connotations of hierarchy and organization."[3]

What we do know for certain about these entities is: 1) how the Bible describes their actions, and 2) the place they are located.

THIS PRESENT DARKNESS

According to Scripture (John 8:44; 2 Cor. 4:4; Rev. 20:10, for example) what is the enemy's most obvious calling card?

The express purpose of Paul's command—"Be strong in the Lord and in the strength of His might" (Eph. 6:10)—is so that we can "stand against the schemes of the devil" (v. 11, CSB). *Schemes* refers to deceptive strategies or tactics. His attacks are always wrapped in the packaging of deception, designed to manipulate the truth about God and about you.

What the enemy wants is to lead you into sin, breaking your fellowship with God—the fellowship between you and the One who provides your true power and strength. Then, weakened and vulnerable, you'll be susceptible to Satan's plans to destroy you. That's why the enemy seeks to stay hidden as much as possible.

So don't believe for one second that the false ideologies of the world have been developed by chance. The evil temptations that appeal to your specific desires are not accidental. The discord and disharmony that threaten your most valuable relationships are not coincidental. The temptations that tug at you during your weakest moments are not uncalculated. They are his deceptive tactics (and that of his evil entourage), specifically designed and personalized to keep you from experiencing abundant life.

Look back at Day 1's lesson and consider the people or circumstances you listed in the oval as being among the most difficult in your life. Prayerfully consider how the enemy's calculated deception may be playing a role in these situations. Record your thoughts in the margin.

HOME COURT ADVANTAGE

All right, so we know this much: Satan's calling card is deception. But Paul also goes to great lengths to draw attention to the place where the enemy and his evil forces are located. Not once but twice, he echoes this important fact in the Book of Ephesians.

According to these verses (Eph. 3:10 and 6:12), where are the enemy and his spiritual forces of darkness located?

The heavenly places. This is the invisible, unseen realm in which the cosmic battle originates and rages, where real activity is even now taking place that directly affects our circumstances. Weapons and artillery that might work when fighting an earthly battle do not work in this realm. Only those weapons divinely sanctioned and authorized by God (which are the ones we're going to learn to use in this study) can have any effect in a battle like this.

So since the enemy is in heavenly places, and the war is raging in heavenly places, and the weapons required for achieving victory are designed to be operational in heavenly places ... it's easy to feel a bit confused and unsure how you could possibly engage in this battle since you are down here on earth. A little lesson about your spiritual location is in order.

Record all the important facts you discover about heavenly places from these verses:

- **Ephesians 1:3**

- **Ephesians 1:20**

- **Ephesians 2:6**

Not only is every spiritual blessing you will ever need for walking in victory in heavenly places, but even right now as you hold this book, you too are seated in heavenly places with Christ at the right hand of the Father.

Pause and let the worship fall over you from that statement. You are not just present in heavenly places; you are sitting down in those heavenly places!

In ancient times, being "seated" was the symbolic posture of a king whose army had already been victorious in battle. Instead of standing, pacing, or worrying himself to death, he would park himself on his throne as a visible statement of his complete and utter triumph.

Christ our King is seated in heavenly places as a proclamation that ultimate victory over the enemy has already been accomplished. And you and I are seated there, too, since we've been made victorious in Christ. Your enemy knows it, and so should you. The cross and the resurrection were the final steps in sealing the claim of victory over his kingdom.

He's been:
- disarmed, embarrassed (Col. 2:15);
- overruled (Eph. 1:20-22);
- mastered (Phil. 2:9-11);
- rendered powerless (Heb. 2:14);
- and all his hard work destroyed (1 John 3:8).

Once you've placed faith in Jesus, you are now transported with Christ to a position of victory. In other words, you have the home court advantage.

So, yes, we still live on earth, and we still have to deal with the physical ailments, environmental evils, and relational hardships of this planet. But because of our spiritual location, we always have hope. And, through Christ, we can bring the victory of heaven into our experience on earth.

Satan knows that he cannot destroy you. The best he can do (and he intends to make full use of it) is to make your time on earth futile and unproductive, to suffocate you with sin, insecurity, fear, and discouragement until you are unable to live freely and fully. He can't "unseat" you, but he can intimidate you and render you ineffective and paralyzed.

If you feel anything like I do, you've had enough. You won't let him have one more moment of victory in your life. Not today. Not on your watch.

As we go through these next six weeks of study, we're going to become more aware than ever of the power that our position in heavenly places affords us. We are also going to learn to access it and use it. Together, we'll start to understand what it means to throw our weight around with the divine strength we've been given and push back the darkness. With every passing day, we'll grow stronger.

Actionable Intel...

> **I HAVE THE HOME COURT ADVANTAGE.**
> #ArmorOfGodStudy

> *As a result, we are no longer to be children, tossed here and there by waves and carried about by every wind of doctrine, by the trickery of men, by craftiness in deceitful scheming (Eph. 4:14).*

WHAT'S IN A NAME?

In Scripture, names were much more than nomenclature. They revealed the character of the person. The same is true for our enemy. An overview of his names reveals his overarching methodology of attack against God's people. Here are some of them.

1. *Satan* **means "the adversary" [of God].** The enemy is antagonistic to the plans and purposes of God. He will always seek to misconstrue and malign the character of God and to thwart the purposes of God (Job 1:6).

2. *Devil* **means "slanderous."** The enemy's intention is to defame and malign the character and intentions of God and others. He will whisper lies in hopes of belittling God's reputation, which in turn will diminish your confidence in God and cause you to mistrust His direction (Matt. 4:1; Eph. 4:25-27).

3. *Lucifer* **means "day star" or "shining one."** The enemy's appearance is attractive, alluring, and charming. Because of this, he can approach you in an appealing way to lure and entice your attention and admiration. This deceptive package will often be the furthest from repulsive or foul, making his handiwork difficult to detect (Isa. 14:12-14; Luke 10:18).

4. *Tempter* **means "one who tempts people for the purpose of enticing them to sin."** The enemy seeks to mislead your passions so that you will seek to fulfill them in perverted, illegitimate ways. He'll intentionally set personalized temptations in your path that are distorted variations of God's gifts to you (Matt. 4:3; 1 Thess. 3:5).

5. *Ruler of the World* **means the enemy's approach is not isolated to individuals.** He has collective cultural and global methods designed to derail entire nations and people groups from God's intended plan. He carefully crafts and proliferates philosophies, doctrines, and moral perspectives across entire demographics in order to steer whole societies away from God (John 12:31; 2 Cor. 4:4).

6. *Prince of the Power of the Air/Prince of Darkness* **means the devil does not work alone.** He is the chief leader of the tribe of dark forces who seek to carry out his purposes in the domain of darkness—a very real, yet invisible realm that affects everything seen and heard in the physical, visible realm (Eph. 2:2; Eph. 6:12).

7. *Accuser* **means "one who condemns."** The enemy seeks to weaken the believer's confidence and influence by conveying condemnation and guilt. He points out and constantly reminds you of sin and mistakes in order to cripple the believer with discouragement and shame (Rev. 12:10).

8. *Father of Lies* **means "liar" and "falsifier."** The enemy's character contains no truth and light. When he speaks and acts, he will always seek to falsify and deceive. He will blatantly and unapologetically misconstrue the truths of your personal reality and circumstance. He will also seek to mislead you with inaccuracies regarding God, His Word, and His plans for you (John 8:44).

DAY 3
LAZY DAYS

There is an enemy. He is real. And he is actively working against you day by day, moment by moment. His goal? To keep you from experiencing the results of the victory that is already yours in Christ.

He knows that you, as a child of God, cannot be destroyed. But he has other goals in the meantime: to distract you, discourage you, divide you from others, and disable you from experiencing everything that is rightfully yours as an adopted member of God's family. He wants to terrorize you until you're miserable and incapable of living in the benefits of a victory that has already been won.

I'm not making this up, nor am I trying to scare you. In fact, you shouldn't be afraid, despite the target drawn in bright red colors on your back. But you'd better be alert and on your guard.

What do you think it looks like to be "on your guard" against the enemy in practical, everyday terms? Record a few ideas.

In our culture, Christianity has become quite comfortable. Coffee shops in church lobbies. Shuttles to the sanctuary from the parking lot on rainy days. Games during youth group on Sunday nights. That's all fine and good.

But don't be lulled to sleep. Don't ever allow the abundance of our culture to dull your alertness or curb the fighting edge you need to defeat your most formidable foe. Refuse to allow comfort and ease to make you apathetic, uninterested, and in some cases, unaware of the battle that is raging all around you.

The lazy days of Christian culture must come to an end. Starting today. Starting with you. Starting with us.

How have you seen Christianity and the general church culture become more characterized by laziness and apathy than activity and alertness?

In what specific ways have you noticed spiritual apathy or indifference in your own life recently?

Consider again the specific person or circumstances you wrote down at the beginning of the week. Which of the following two choices would best describe your approach to this issue within the last month?

- ☐ **Proactive, alert, on guard for the enemy's strategies**
- ☐ **Spiritually disengaged, disinterested, too tired to care**

Based on your selection, how would you describe the results of your approach?

Our enemy celebrates lethargic Christian living. When we're giving up on relationships, disregarding the purity of our reputations, yielding to our sinful appetites without putting up much, if any, resistance, he can basically go unchecked. Wreak havoc in the lives of God's people. Ultimately, he can keep the church from achieving the purposes of God. Our laziness works to his great advantage, practically rolling out the red carpet for his entrance into the unlocked doors of our indifference and despondency. He's hardly going to pass up an opening like that.

That's why Satan works so hard to beat you down with discouragement. Lie to you about who God is, causing you to doubt the Lord's all-good intentions toward you. Hammer you with accusations that place a burden of shame and guilt on your shoulders too heavy to carry. Trick you into thinking your situation will never change, and that God doesn't hear you or care when you call out to Him. Soon your fire of passion starts to burn low, and you grow lackluster. Disinterested. Your spiritual armor goes unworn and unused.

Bingo.

Now you're exactly where the enemy wants you—where you no longer want to fight for peace in your relationships, where you no longer believe you can be restored, no longer hope for healing in your body, no longer see any path to freedom from your addictions, and where you just don't see the purpose in praying anymore, so you don't. You don't ask or seek or knock. You don't take advantage of your heavenly-places position and benefits package that comes from having "every spiritual blessing" in the universe handed to you as an inheritance as God's child.

Maybe you kind of don't care anymore. You're not even sure you want to. But through prayer, you can get your "want-to" back.

TAKE ACTION

Write out Ephesians 6:10-11. You can copy it directly from page 7 if you'd like. When you are finished, underline all the action verbs and phrases.

Now, turn to page 7 and underline the verbs you see in verses 12-19.

The Book of Ephesians is a delicate mix between God's gifts and our responsibilities. The first three chapters speak to the identity and status God freely gives to believers in Christ. But beginning in the fourth chapter, the tone shifts to the believer's responsibility to act.

First, the indicatives—everything that's been accomplished for us in Christ because of the victory He's already won. Then, the imperatives—how we are supposed to use them so that we can actually receive and experience the tangible, long-term effects of this victory in our practical, everyday living.

Simply put: believe and receive first; then use what you've been given.

In your own words, what is the difference between indicatives and imperatives? Between the first half of Ephesians and the second half? Explain.

Indicative: adj. A mood of verb that states a fact or truth

Imperative: adj. A mood of verb that denotes a command

A good example of this balance is clearly seen in Ephesians 6:10-11. Paul's command to "be strong in the Lord" is in the passive tense, meaning that strength is something God gives you, something you receive. You could actually read this phrase as "Be strengthened in the Lord." God Himself infusing strength into you.

Three overarching indicatives in Ephesians:
1) Headship of Christ
2) The cornerstone is Christ
3) Unity in Christ

But then, in the very next verse, Paul described how we put ourselves in position to receive this strength: "Put on the full armor of God." By putting on the armor, we activate the strengthening process. It's like plugging in your phone charger. You can count on your phone to hold a charge, but only if you've taken the initiative to plug it in. We will never realize the fullness of God's strength in our lives if we ignore the spiritual protection He offers. It's always available, but we must "plug in" if we want to access it.

Have you ever failed to "plug in" to God's power? What happened? What did you learn from that situation?

This call to "put on" the armor denotes both urgency and resolution. It's as if Paul is saying there's no time to waste. You must put on the armor now. Daily. Consistently. Faithfully. If we want our resolve to be strengthened and our stance made firm, we need to realize that spiritual warfare doesn't take a day off. We must choose now to engage each of the individual pieces of armor if we expect to see their full effect in spiritual warfare.

What's the difference between the passive command to "be strong in the Lord" and the active command to "put on the whole armor of God"? How does one affect the other?

Philippians 2:12b-13 is a combination of active and passive commands. Read it in the margin and see if you can detect them. Write them below
   Active:

   Passive:

Work out your salvation with fear and trembling; for it is God who is at work in you, both to will and to work for His good pleasure (Phil. 2:12b-13).

Even though the previous question was intended to help you spot both the active and passive sides of authentic gospel living, don't miss the beautiful, encouraging message of verse 13. Read it again. God is working in you right now to help you want to get your want-to back.

WAKE-UP CALL

The call to victorious Christian living is a wake-up call out of laziness, urging you to rise up and take serious action. The strength you need for resisting and standing firm depends on it. Satan and the demons of darkness are hoping you'll be disengaged and disinterested instead of alert, aware, and active.

Record the commands to action described in 1 Peter 5:8. Why do we need to respond this way? What happens when we don't?

Lazy, lethargic Christianity can no longer be an option. Not when an angry, hungry lion is out there stalking you, waiting for a moment of weakness or distraction, itching to pounce. Not if you want to experience the full bounty of life in Christ.

During these next six weeks, the apostle Paul is going to call us to an active Christian lifestyle that requires a firm resolve and forward movement—in prayer, righteousness, and faith. It demands we get serious, strategic, and intentional.

Come on now—it's time to wake up.

Actionable Intel...

DAY 4
BAIT SELECTION

My sons and I enjoy fishing. Our neighbor's pond across the street affords us ample opportunity to toss in a line and hope for a few small sun perch. I'm no serious fisherman, mind you. No live worms for me. Our bait is leftover hot dog meat from the refrigerator. It usually does the trick ... at least at the pond at our house.

But last summer we visited a Christian camp that circled a massive lake, stocked with larger varieties like bass and catfish. My boys and I, of course, couldn't pass up the chance to try for the bigger catch. But we weren't having much luck, until a man fishing near us saw my sad excuse for bait and offered to exchange it for something better.

He dislodged a tiny perch that one of my sons had just reeled in, affixed a much sturdier hook on the line, and then did something shocking: gashed that poor little fish right onto the hook. As bait!

"Try it now," he said.

We all were thoroughly flabbergasted and grossed out. (Actually, that was just me. My boys were thrilled.) But sure enough, when we cast that perch into the water, my 11-year-old was soon reeling in a five-pound bass.

A change in bait changed everything.

The enemy is a master at choosing the right kind of bait to snag you. Let that sink in. Sure, he uses some overarching, one-size-fits-all tactics to disarm God's people in general, but he doesn't use just one type of bait for every person, or even the same type of bait for any one individual over time. No, he carefully considers and calculates your current situation, taking into account your weaknesses and strengths, your interests and tendencies, your history and past abuses, everything. Then, using this available information, he crafts a specific strategy to hook you and reel you in.

Don't believe it? If you look carefully, you'll notice that the battles the devil wages against you—especially the most acute, consistent

Detecting the enemy's strategies is the first step in defeating him. See Digging Deeper 2 on page 34 for more insight on the primary ways he attacks us.

ones—reveal intimate knowledge of who you are and the precise pressure points where you can most easily be taken down. Random accident? Lucky guess? I don't think so. These areas of greatest fear and anxiety in your life are clues to some important spiritual information. They reveal, among other things, that Satan has put a personalized strategy in place to defeat you. It's been crafted by the enemy himself, someone who knows from experience how best to take advantage of your areas of vulnerability.

Consider again some of the people or circumstances you listed in that oval at the beginning of the week. In what ways, if any, might these issues reveal how the enemy has personalized his bait to hook you? How do one or more of these people or situations press a specific "hot button" for you?

Once you become aware of the enemy's strategy and begin to see his handiwork beneath the surface of your most trying life circumstances, you can not only begin to target the right culprit, but you can also start anticipating some of his attacks. Then you can be prepared beforehand, giving him little room to make you a casualty of war.

Listen to me: Satan is tricky, but he is not original or particularly creative. He's always had the same basic game plan. And if you're watching, you'll see that sometimes the areas where he's targeting you are the ones you'd already expect. By being proactive in prayer and ready with your spiritual armor, you'll be able to detect his secret plans before the attack unfolds, and you can sabotage his efforts to deceive and disable you.

TARGET PRACTICE

I'm not saying the devil is not a formidable enemy. I'm just saying we give him far too much credit for being impossible to defend against or defeat. One of the reasons he gets the best of us so often is because we make his job way too easy for him. So let's try making it a little easier on ourselves instead. We can boil down his playbook to just a couple of main attack strategies. And to decode them, all you need to do is ask yourself two questions.

1) IN WHAT WAY(S) DO I POSE THE BIGGEST THREAT TO THE ENEMY AND HIS PURPOSES?

The enemy will always seek to hinder you in areas where you're keeping his goals from being accomplished. Are you particularly vocal about your faith? Then he may agitate fear or insecurity in you so you'll keep your mouth closed. Are you committed to sexual purity? Then he will try to detour you away from that commitment with false promises. Predictably, Satan wants to cripple you in the area of your life where doing so will most directly defame God and hinder His church.

Think about the person or circumstance you wrote down earlier—how might the enemy interpret this area of your life as being of benefit to the kingdom of God, and therefore target it for destruction?

Here's a recent example from my own life: One of the most exciting (and shocking) things the Lord has ever allowed me to do in ministry was participate in a movie project called *War Room*. I was stunned speechless when the directors, Stephen and Alex Kendrick, called to see if I would consider acting in it. Me? An actress? I laughed out loud. Like, for real. But when I found out the message of the movie was about the power of prayer and standing firm against the enemy, I reconsidered.

Several weeks before filming started, one of them sent me an email, detailing some ways to prepare for the experience. Here's a portion of it:

> *"We have had spiritual attacks on all of our movies. The theme of this movie is on calling the body of Christ among the nations to their knees in strategic prayer. The devil is not happy about that. Now that you are joining the team, don't be surprised if the enemy drops unusual family, relational, or health problems in your life. Don't worry. Just prepare. God is greater than anything the enemy attempts."*

Bottom line: anticipate the enemy to hit you in the area of your greatest influence. And, boy, were they right! The enemy came after my family with a vengeance. Disagreements. Short fuses. Hot feelings. Even though I had been warned, I didn't fully realize how that summer of on-site shooting would affect some of our relational dynamics. Never has our family endured as difficult a stretch as during the summer of shooting this movie—which, among other things, dealt with preserving unity in one's family!

That's just the way our enemy plays. Dirty, but not without being decipherable. Consider where you're feeling the strongest these days. And expect to take some hits in those particular areas.

2) WHAT ARE MY FLESH'S TENDENCIES, INNATE PASSIONS, AND WEAKNESSES?

Every human being has tendencies—a bent toward particular tastes and interests, passions and curiosities, some good but maybe some bad. Or at least sensitive, perhaps embarrassing, things we don't like others to know about us. And those predispositions and weaknesses are the ones the enemy will seek to exploit. Whether they come from your upbringing, your inborn personality, or vulnerabilities created by events in your life, these appetites of yours influence how Satan targets you. And when you combine these predispositions and weaknesses with his knowledge of just the right time to tease them out, you know as much or more than he does about how he may be planning to attack you at your most susceptible moments.

One of my sons, for example, has always been prone toward fear and anxiety. Ever since he was a small child, he's leaned toward this emotional response. Knowing this, I've been very specific in praying for him, even when he was a tiny baby. I routinely ask the Holy Spirit to instill courage within him, to be a wall of protection against the enemy's attempts to exploit his bent in this direction. I also speak God's Word out loud over him regarding his position and power in Christ. Fear is an opening Satan will use to get at my son's heart to cripple him if we let him—if we don't know where to be watching.

What about you? If addiction runs in your family, you know the enemy will likely be looking to destroy you through what's perhaps a sensitivity in your mind toward addiction. If sexual impurity has been a part of your history, he'll want to keep that temptation alive while sending enticing offers to lead you astray.

Revisit your answer from a moment ago about your inclinations and tendencies. Now that you've considered the insight they give you into Satan's strategies against you, can you think of any more? May as well be honest here. The more authentic you are, the more specifically you'll be able to zero in on the enemy's plans.

What practical parameters can you put around your life to safeguard yourself from the enemy's attempts to bait you in these areas? Be specific.

Keep a close eye on your areas of greatest strength and weakness. They are likely the places where you can expect Satan to target his attacks against you. When you know where to look, you can see him coming from a mile away. He's really not that clever. He's just cunning.

But his number's up with you and me. Be ready. Be prayed up. Stand your guard.

Actionable Intel...

THE ENEMY'S STRATEGIES

After polling a large cross section of people, asking them to reveal the primary ways the enemy attacks their lives, I found several common categories defined their responses. Below are ten of the enemy's favorite strategies to use against God's children as they pursue abundant life in Christ.

Strategy #1—Against Your Passion

He seeks to dim your whole desire for prayer, dull your interest in spiritual things, and downplay the potency of your most strategic weapons (Eph. 6:10-20).

Strategy #2—Against Your Focus

He disguises himself and manipulates your perspective so you end up focusing on the wrong culprit, directing your weapons at the wrong enemy (2 Cor. 11:14).

Strategy #3—Against Your Identity

He magnifies your insecurities, leading you to doubt what God says about you and to disregard the tools and blessings He's given you (Eph. 1:17-19).

Strategy #4—Against Your Family

Satan wants to destroy your family and will do all he can to divide your home, rendering it chaotic, restless, and unfruitful (Gen. 3:1-7).

Strategy #5—Against Your Confidence

He constantly reminds you of your past mistakes and sins, hoping to convince you that you're under God's judgment rather than under the blood (Rev. 12:10).

Strategy #6—Against Your Calling

He amplifies fear, worry, and anxiety until they're the loudest voices in your head, causing you to deem the adventure of following God too risky to attempt (Josh. 14:8).

Strategy #7—Against Your Purity

He tries to tempt you toward certain sins, convincing you that you can tolerate them without risking consequence, knowing they'll only wedge distance between you and God (Isa. 59:1-2).

Strategy #8—Against Your Rest and Contentment

He hopes to overload your life and schedule, pressuring you to constantly push beyond your limits, never feeling permission to say no (Deut. 5:15).

Strategy #9—Against Your Heart

He uses every opportunity to keep old wounds fresh in mind, knowing that anger, hurt, bitterness, and unforgiveness will continue to roll the damage forward (Heb. 12:15).

Strategy #10—Against Your Relationships

He creates disruption and disunity within your circle of friends and within the shared community of the body of Christ, the church (1 Tim. 2:8).

DAY 5

STRATEGY SESSION

So, what's your plan? Do you have one? Your enemy certainly does. He's been studying you, baiting you—zeroing in on your tendencies, habits, and appetites. His attacks have not been random or unsystematic. They are highly calculated and precise, ready to be waged against you in heavenly places.

On this final day of our first week of study, you and I can see Satan much more clearly for who he really is and what he's been doing to discourage and disarm us. So now it's time to compose our own strategy, to cut him off at the pass. That's right—a plan to sabotage his efforts—because we can't just go barreling into this fight blindly. We can't just throw something up against the wall and hope it sticks. We need to craft a blueprint for our success.

A strategy for war.

LET US PRAY

Today, we've come to what will be the highlight of each of our weeks together. This is where the proverbial rubber meets the road, and you begin to advance against the enemy's activity in your life. This is how you'll begin to Take. Stuff. Back.

In Jesus' name.

Listen to me carefully: Prayer is the mechanism that brings down the power of heaven into your experience. It is the divinely authorized method that activates your spiritual armor and makes it effective. Prayer alerts the enemy to your awareness of his intentions while safeguarding you from his attacks. It is his kryptonite. It is what weakens and unravels all his ploys against you.

I believe I can say it as bluntly as this: Unless prayer is a vital and thriving part of your life, you will never achieve spiritual victory. No matter how many times you go through this study, no matter how many Christian camps or mission trips you participate in, or how often you go to church, you will forever be spinning your wheels until you're grounded in prayer. Prayer is what connects you with the heavenly places. And that is always where spiritual battles are won.

So, starting today—and at the end of every week we have together—here's what I want you to do: Compile the various bits of "Actionable Intel" you've been gathering from your week of Bible study, open up a journal or notebook, and begin to craft a personalized prayer strategy for your life—one that's grounded in thanksgiving and gratitude for what God has already done, and also punctuated with promises from His own Word. Then ask—yes, ask—the Lord to open your spiritual eyes, to alert you to the enemy's intentions, and to give you the proactive courage to lay down any physical weapons you have been trusting rather than the ones He has provided, ones that really work! Don't speak in generic terms; put your own issues, loved ones, and needs on paper. Then use this list as your reminder to pray against the enemy and every demonic assault he's planned against you.

Look at the verses from Ephesians 6 below. Underline every instance where you see any variation of the word "pray."

> *"With all prayer and petition pray at all times in the Spirit, and with this in view, be on the alert with all perseverance and petition for all the saints, and pray on my behalf ..." (vv. 18–19a).*

Turns out, there aren't only six pieces of armor, as most people think. There are seven. Prayer is the linchpin that holds our armor together. It is what activates all the other pieces and fortifies you as a soldier in battle. It is the device that empowers and "charges up" every other piece so they can be used effectively against the enemy. Without prayer—I say it again—your armor cannot and will not be infused with the power that only God's Spirit can give.

When Paul said to "pray at all times," he didn't mean time in a general sense. The word translated *at all times* in this verse is *kairos*, which refers to specific times, precise occasions, and particular events. In spiritual warfare, as we detect enemy activity and deploy the different pieces of armor, our prayers need to be fervent and specific, strategic and personal. Tied to specific needs that arise at that specific occasion. That's the kind of prayer that energizes the armor of God for maximum effectiveness.

Your prayers only need to be authentic and heartfelt. There's no specific length, and prayer doesn't have to use big words or sound like poetry. It's just a conversation with your Father. You're not trying to impress anybody. Just be real with God. Then—and I'm serious about this—tear your prayer out of your notebook and post it somewhere where you will see it every day as a reminder to pray about it. That might be on your bathroom mirror, on the wall in your room, or inside the front cover of a notebook for school.

The devil is going to be sorry he ever messed with you because you're a person devoted to fervent, precise, effective prayer who plans to shut him down, IN JESUS' NAME. He's been gathering his intel on you and striking at places where you pose the biggest threat to his work. Has he been hitting you where you're weak or simply unaware?

Well, now, you're gathering some intel to use against him.

So, grab a pen.

Open up your journal.

Write.

And then, pray.

Refer to page 192 if you need prayer guidelines to help you get started.

THE BELT OF TRUTH

Think about the word trustworthy. What qualities or characteristics make someone or something trustworthy?

What are some things you've seen people put their trust in? What actions or behaviors help you to know what others place their trust in? Explain.

People trust a lot of things to show them what's true. Other people. What they can see or hear. How they feel. Previous experiences. But when it comes to defeating the enemy's power in our lives, victory doesn't lie in any of those things. It lies in the truth, the whole truth and nothing but the truth.

Turn to page 7 and read Ephesians 6:13-14 again. Then read it aloud from several different translations.

While different translations of the Bible may use different phrases, the message remains the same. The first piece of armor, the very first action Paul identified for us and commanded us to use in order to stand firm against the attacks of the enemy, is the belt of truth.

Why do you think truth is so important when it comes to standing firm against Satan's attacks?

The enemy does not take a blanket, generalized approach when he attacks us in the body of Christ. Whether directed at an individual or a group of people, His approach is always specific. He has personalized, individualized, targeted attacks planned for you and planned for me. He is studying you. He knows what your weaknesses are. He knows what would cause you to be crippled by peacelessness and anxiety. And he zeros in on what he knows will work for you. But there is always one principle that is present in every last one of his attacks: deception. Deception is the mark of the enemy.

Read John 8:44. List everything this verse teaches you about Satan and his character.

Lying is Satan's native language. He can't do anything but lie; it's in his very character. And if we want to be on guard against the enemy, then we have to remember that deception is his disguise. He is the master illusionist, better than Harry Houdini ever was at causing us to think something is real when it isn't.

Sometimes the enemy is obvious in his attacks against us, but most of the time he isn't. He's cunning and sinister, hiding his true intentions in deception. Sometimes we don't even know it's him! He creates an illusion that looks like truth and even seems good or in our best interest, but it isn't.

How would you define an illusion? Write it below in your own words.

An illusion is something that deceives by producing a false or misleading impression of reality. In other words, Satan promises something that looks good and right, but actually isn't. It's an illusion, a mirage, bait and switch, pulling the wool over your eyes. And that's how the enemy operates.

One of the ways Satan does this is by making us think God does not mean exactly what He says.

How have you or someone you know experienced this? Can you think of some examples of this in Scripture? Explain.

A good example is found in the very first pages of the Bible. Read Genesis 3:1-4 aloud.

The devil's deceptive tactic against Eve was to cause her to question God's motive and twist what God had said. He'll do the same to us. He loves to make us think we're not really who God has called us to be in Scripture. He's the one who influences us to think the most unhealthy, toxic dating relationships in our lives have value. Satan will lead us to think that habit or behavior really isn't that big of a deal, so we continue to engage in it day after day and don't even know it's whittling away at our very souls.

That's deception. The enemy deludes us until we think we're walking in truth when we're actually not. And so what we need is an unchangeable, objective standard that is outside of ourselves and gives us a clear perspective on what's happening in our lives.

My family and I travel a lot. One of the things that always happens no matter what airport I'm at, is that when I go through security, I always have to check-in with the agent first. I hand him my ID, and he looks at it carefully, comparing the photo with my face. But the agent doesn't stop there. The agent always takes my license and passes it under a special light that will reveal if it's authentic. These agents do not trust in what they can see. They do not trust in how they feel. They do not trust in their previous experience. They always ultimately depend on the light.

We have a light also. Read aloud Proverbs 3:5-6. What should be the unchanging standard in our lives as believers?

Now read Ephesians 5:13. Fill in the blank.
God's truth is the _____.

Satan's suggestions can never stand up against the *light* of God's Holy Word. As warriors, as believers who possess the power to defeat Satan and are on to his deceptive tactics, we must pass every decision, every action, every behavior under the light of God's Word.

Read Joshua 24:15. What does this verse mean for your life in what you've learned today? Explain.

In the first century Roman army, the belt was actually the very first thing a soldier would put on. It resembled the back brace a UPS® or FedEx® driver wears today, a wide band that stretches across the entire midsection and provides extra stability at their core. The soldier's armor weighed close to 70 pounds. Without the extra strength and fortification the belt provided, the soldiers would easily buckle under the pressure. They wouldn't be able to withstand the pressure of the armor they wore or be able to go into battle. In Ephesians 6, Paul correlates *truth* to the soldier's belt.

What does this teach you about the importance of God's Word in your life?

We live in a world of relativity. Everybody's got their own truth. But for us, as people who are committed to girding ourselves in truth, we must pledge our allegiance to uphold, to encourage, to support, and to affirm God's standard as the standard for our lives. God's Word is the deciding factor for the choices we make and the places we go. It defines how we choose to live. It fortifies and stabilizes us in changing times. We have to determine that we will not just read the Bible, but that it will serve as our standard for living.

We must be people who strap on the belt of truth. When we do so, it …

- **Allows us to _____ _____ against the schemes of the devil (Eph. 6:11).**

- **Makes us truly _____ so we can experience the abundant life we were created for (John 8:32).**

Read over Numbers 13:1-33 as a group. God told the Israelites He was giving them the promised land, yet how many of those spies actually got to go in?

The answer is disheartening: two. Only two—Joshua and Caleb—were willing to affirm the truth of God above what they saw with their natural eyes and what they heard with their physical ears. There were 10 who never moved forward into the promised land because they didn't allow the truth of God to override their feelings.

God has gone before you. He has prepared beforehand good works so that we can walk in them (Eph. 2:10). All we have to do is put on the belt of truth and submit our feelings, our lives, and our desires to Him.

Gird yourself in the truth. This is where the victory begins.

DAY 1
STRENGTHEN YOUR CORE

Fitness gyms are packed with people lifting weights, riding spin bikes, walking on treadmills, and whirring away at elliptical machines. People are firming muscles, shedding pounds, and expanding their lung capacities.

But even with all the equipment, classes, and memberships, most workout programs neglect a key part of the body: the core. A person can be dedicated to his or her exercise regimen, yet not be actively growing stronger in the one place where he or she needs it most.

Your core is the area around your torso and hips, comprised of the abdominal muscle groups. It's the central link in the chain that connects the lower and upper parts of your body, enabling all your limbs and movements to work together in harmony. Every motion you make—whether sweeping the floor or swinging a golf club—requires support from this area. A strong core helps with your balance, your stability, your resistance to injury, and your stamina over time and under pressure. In fact, as the aging process sets in, a weak core could mean the difference between being able to walk upright or being relegated to a chair. The condition of your core affects everything.

Skim the previous paragraph. Underline the benefits of a strong core.

In light of the following verses, consider the benefits you underlined in relation to your spiritual life. Write them beside the reference below with a corresponding theme.

- **Ephesians 6:13-14a**

- **Ephesians 2:13-17**

- **Ephesians 4:14**

- **James 1:2-4**

Based on these passages, what makes these attributes and benefits so important for spiritual health? Explain.

In what ways have you noticed these attributes missing in the Christian community? Be specific.

What about in your personal life? Are there any particular ways you are experiencing imbalance, instability, weakness, or internal discord right now? Describe below.

CORE SUPPORT

OK, I'm not trying to restructure your exercise program. But having a strong, well-supported core seems to be what Paul had in mind when he began crafting his list of spiritual armor.

His main image is based largely on the imagery of the Divine Warrior from Isaiah 59. But we can still learn a lot about the role and purpose of this armor by considering the Roman legionary—which was seemingly always present in Jewish culture during Paul's day. The pieces of armor listed in Ephesians 6 are arranged in the same order in which a Roman soldier would've put them on to prepare for battle.

Turn to page 65 to read more about the Divine Warrior: Digging Deeper 3

Turn to page 7 and look at Ephesians 6:10-18. List the pieces of armor in order, as they appear.

1.

2.

3.

4.

5.

6.

7.   **Prayer**

LEGION. Gk. legeōn (from Lat. legio), used four times in the New Testament, was the main division of the Roman army, and comprised between 4,000 and 6,000 men. It was divided into ten cohorts and these in turn into six centuries each.[1]

Looking at the first entry on your list and keeping in mind the significance of the core, why do you think putting on this piece of equipment first would've been critical for a soldier?

While some translations render Paul's original wording in Ephesians 6:14 as *belt,* this English term actually conjures up an incorrect image. The phrase in this verse literally says, "Stand, having girded your loins …" No real mention of a belt there. Not even a specific description of any piece of equipment at all. But we can deduce Paul's meaning by noting the Roman soldier's attire and seeing that the belt is used for the purpose of girding his "loins."

What specific spiritual attribute did Paul connect to this piece of equipment?

Why do you think this attribute (truth) must come first in any successful spiritual warfare against the enemy?

Generally speaking, our society isn't one that takes strong, firm stands on truth. Even the church, sadly, too often fails to hold clear views on right living and God-honoring choices. Many people who call themselves Christians today don't have a strong core belief system to govern their lives. They don't frame their decisions around the truth of God's Word, aren't stable and sturdy in their convictions, are too easily injured and wounded by others, and buckle under pressure rather than standing tough and persevering.

But starting today, you and I will be doing things differently. Even if you admit to being fairly spineless up until now in how you've handled the circumstances of life, your approach is about to change. Honestly, all of us can benefit from strengthening our cores and making ourselves tough and durable for the long haul.

That's just the truth.

And that's just where we're headed next.

STANDARD BEARER

A Roman soldier "girded his loins" with something more akin to a girdle than a belt. (A manly one, I'm sure.) Most scholars agree that more than any other piece of the soldier's clothing or equipment, this girdle—with its intricate decor and elaborate buckles—distinguished a soldier from a civilian. It wasn't some optional, secondary accessory. It was a strategic, primary focal point of his attire. Think of those wide lumbar braces that UPS® and FedEx® workers wear around their waists when carrying heavy packages. The sturdy, leather girdle of the Roman soldier was made to reach around the torso and provide essential support while he performed the quick, demanding movements of war.

Truth is your core support. It provides the essential backing you need when you're in the midst of spiritual war.

Remember, the enemy's overarching device is deception. He shades reality with enticing and alluring colors, seducing us away from black-and-white principles. He cultivates fantasies, causing temporary and insignificant things to somehow appear immensely valuable and favorable. He hides consequences in the fine print while highlighting only the parts that appeal to our shortsighted, self-gratifying flesh. His packaging is so clever that unless we know what's true—I mean *really know it,* know it at our core—we easily fall prey to his ploys.

What are some of the most clever illusions you've seen the enemy craft in your own life or in the life of a friend? What lies does he most often tell you?

What were some consequences the enemy glossed over or tucked in the "fine print"?

How would you define *truth*? Write your definition below.

Truth is God's opinion on any matter.

The definition in the margin should help you as you consider the definition of *truth*. Think about a time or times in your life when your desires were aligned with what you know to be true from God's Word. Do you usually ...

- ☐ **do what you want to do and pray for forgiveness later?**
- ☐ **grit your teeth and force your actions to God's standard?**
- ☐ **try to massage God's Word so it fits in with your desires?**
- ☐ **cry out in prayer and try to ride it out patiently, trustingly?**
- ☐ **talk to somebody about what you're struggling with?**
- ☐ **do something else entirely?**

My sons recently became interested in guitar. And after making sure this was something they would follow through with, I purchased a pre-owned instrument for them to share and signed them all up for online lessons. But their first bit of instruction came from a friend of ours, Natalie, who was visiting our house one day. An experienced guitar player, she could tell with one strum that the strings were out of tune. So starting with the top string—the E, getting it exactly on pitch—she worked through all the other strings, basing their individual tones off the accuracy of the first one. Once the standard of that first note was set in place, everything else became balanced and in harmony; it became music.

Your word is truth (Ps. 119:160).

Truth—which we could basically define as God's opinion on any matter—is our standard. Our E string. Truth is who God is and what He says it is, best summed up for us within the Person of Jesus Christ.

God's truth. Biblical truth. Without concrete allegiance to and affirmation with this truth—with real truth—you're left weak and susceptible to things that may look right and sound right yet actually aren't. But with the standard of truth in place, you can adjust everything else in your life—your ambitions, choices, and feelings; your mind, will, and emotions—until all of it is "tuned" correctly. When you have a strong, stable, well-supported core, you can't easily be led astray by the enemy's clever lies. Gird yourself with truth, and you're on guard from the word "go."

TELL ME HOW

How, then, are you supposed to put on this belt of truth? You uphold and affirm the standard—the truth and boundaries set by God in Scripture. You commit yourself to them, live by them, and resolve to teach them to others.

- You daily, systematically, and repeatedly begin letting God help you align your decisions and responses—even your attitudes and ambitions—with His benchmark of truth.
- You continually learn about the character and purposes of God—both from the Bible and from His Spirit. Then you unapologetically synchronize your convictions, even when you find it difficult or unpopular to do so.
- You filter every circumstance, personally and culturally, through the prism of His Word instead of merely leaning on your feelings, political correctness, or the opinions of others.

Truth becomes your starting place, and then everything else begins falling into a much better place.

Read Deuteronomy 6:4-9. Consider the proactive planning and determination it would take to fulfill the mandate outlined there in your own life. How could you implement a strategy to do so this week? Jot down some ideas below.

I will not, I cannot, make the assumption that just because you're involved in this study you're in full, wholehearted agreement with the principle of today's lesson. Just because you read the Bible doesn't mean you've chosen it as your standard for living—any more than a person with a gym membership is necessarily committed to using the equipment in the gym. The real test comes when the ideals and philosophies of our culture swing in the opposite direction, and yet we choose to stand strong and firm on the unchanging standard of God. The time has come for us to be people girded in truth.

Actionable Intel...

DAY 2
TRUTH CHECKUP

I recently learned that I need to start incorporating some strength training into my exercise routine. So I asked around to figure out what the best core strengthening exercises would be for me. When I saw them demonstrated, they didn't look too tough. So I dove in enthusiastically … for about two minutes. That's when I realized how weak my core actually was. Up until then I thought I was pretty strong. But when I started to proactively focus on the areas of weakness in my core, I realized how much work I needed to do to strengthen it.

Your enemy is looking for weaknesses—for loopholes in your resolve that he can take advantage of and exploit. But if you aren't even aware that your commitment to truth in some areas is flimsy, you don't even have a way to do a sit-up, much less a way to keep standing up.

So today, I want you to consider the telltale signs of a weak spiritual core and take an accurate inventory of specific areas that need attention in your life. Get your game face on.

SIGNS OF A WEAK CORE

There are three main indicators that help diagnose and expose weakness in a person's physical core. And by looking at these physical conditions, we can gain spiritual insight as we consider how to become believers who are strengthened and well-supported by the belt of truth.

1. POOR POSTURE

A strong core enables you to stand straighter and keep standing straighter for longer periods of time. Not only that, but the stronger your core, the less likely you'll be to buckle under pressure when carrying heavy loads. A person with a weak core, however, will find his or her shoulders curving and sagging as the aging process sets in.

List key words from the previous paragraph that describe the early signs of a weak core.

Choose one Old Testament and one New Testament passage from the selections below. Write down the side effects of a life that's not girded in truth from the verses you choose.

Old Testament:
- **Genesis 3:6,16-19**
- **Numbers 20:7-8,11-12**
- **Psalm 106:13-15**
- **Jonah 1:1-4**

New Testament:
- **Romans 1:21,24-32**
- **Romans 2:6-9**
- **Ephesians 4:14,18-19**

Now, prayerfully answer the following questions:
Would you currently describe your spiritual posture as upright? If so, what are the indicators of this? If not, how would you describe it and why?

How have you noticed a change in your spiritual posture over time?

When do you find it particularly difficult to keep your spiritual backbone straight? Check as many as apply.
☐ When under pressure from others to conform
☐ When put on the spot to defend my faith or opinion
☐ When carrying the extra weight of difficulty and struggle
☐ Other:

2. INJURY PRONE

The muscles of your core hold your spine in place. When the core is weak, any strenuous activity will cause your backbone to move around more, leaving it unprotected, making the body increasingly susceptible to injury.

Rewrite the second sign of a weak core in your own words.

According to Ephesians 4:26-27, what does the enemy often use to gain opportunity for infiltrating a person's life?

Being injury prone is not only hard on joints and muscles; it's also hard on hearts and relationships. Sensitivity to taking offense is one of the key ways Satan traps believers in his web of deception.

When we are easily wounded and hurt by the words and actions of other people, and then choose to nurse those wounds instead of offering forgiveness and grace, we provide the enemy ample opportunity to plant a root of bitterness in our hearts—a root that's sure to bear rotten fruit for many years to come.

The fruit of offense can be staggering: jealousy, outrage, hatred, anger, just to name a few. We know from Scripture, of course, that not all anger is sin. But when we persist in harboring anger, it can easily take over our lives and control us. Anger is often based on a distortion of the facts. We've forgotten we are accepted in Him no matter what others think or say. That we, as infinitely worse offenders against Him, have still been the recipients of His grace. And as His children, we should extend grace to others.

Wouldn't that be how "truth" would interpret and navigate the situation?

On a scale of 1–5, how easily do you ...

... feel injured and wounded by the words or actions of others?

1	2	3	4	5

... forgive and get over past hurts, put them behind you, and move forward?

1	2	3	4	5

... make other people feel comfortable around you, rather than needing to tiptoe around you for fear of hurting your feelings?

1	2	3	4	5

In the course of a month, how often do you "let the sun go down on your anger"?

3. BODY FATIGUE

Even if your core itself doesn't show overt signs of weakness, its flaws can manifest themselves in other muscle groups. When the core isn't well supported, it's unable to supply the level of strength you need for other body movements.

Underline the last sentence in the previous paragraph.

When you're standing firmly on the truth of God as revealed in His Word—when His truth is at the core of your existence—strength flows into every other area of your life. All your movements and activities (school, church, relationships, sports) bear witness to the power of God at work in you. So even when facing a challenge, you still feel the full weight and wind of God's Spirit reverberating behind you.

On the flip side, however—when you're not girded by the truth of God— the lackluster, exhausting, unfulfilling nature of your relationship with Him leeches out into everything else you engage in.

From the list of adjectives below, choose a word or two to describe how you feel when engaged in each of these areas of your life:

- **School**

- **Family**

- **Church**

- **Hobbies or Sports**

---

tired · energized · motivated · drained · insecure · hopeful
· fulfilled · inspired · discouraged · self-conscious ·
attentive · flexible · bored · frightened · capable · happy

Which of your ongoing frustrations in any of these areas might possibly be connected to your negligence or rejection of a truth from God's Word?

TRUTH QUOTIENT

Based on your self-assessment from today's lesson, how would you rate the strength of your spiritual core? Each of these three indicators—posture, resilience, stamina—can clue you in to your current status. And even though striving to strengthen your core can be difficult at first—just like when exercising your physical core—you'll find renewed incentive over time as you start to ...

- walk uprightly for longer periods of time;
- stay strong, even when under pressure and strain;
- become able to absorb criticism without taking offense;
- feel less uncomfortable and awkward with your convictions;
- be spiritually rejuvenated, refreshed, girded with power and strength.

You'll no longer be weak and "led on by various impulses" (2 Tim. 3:6), but instead will be held steady and strong by the belt of God's truth. You'll not only know where your enemy is likely to strike (as we studied last week), but you'll be packed with the muscle tone to hold him off. I think you're looking stronger already.

Actionable Intel...

DAY 3

THE HANGER

The Roman soldier's belt or girdle served several purposes. One was to add support and strength to his core, as we've already discussed. But another purpose was equally important: the belt secured several additional pieces of his armor and kept them solidly in place.

His sword and dagger, for example, were attached there for easy access. The heavy breastplate—which protected the soldier's heart and vital organs—connected to the girdle as well. Also, as you learned during the group discussion, this is where the soldier tucked his tunic to keep it from tripping him up in battle. So the girdle did three things:

1. Gave support to the core
2. Held and stabilized other key pieces of armor
3. Secured the tunic

Yesterday we dealt with #1. Today we'll consider #2 and #3.

HOLD IT TOGETHER

A soldier without his girdle was like a policeman without his holster. Nowhere to keep anything. Think of the disastrous ripple effects. Without it, the legionary would need to carry his sword in one hand and his dagger in the other—and hope and pray he didn't need a third hand for something else ... like maybe keeping his shield up? Or using his fists to fight with? Or reaching for another weapon? Furthermore, without anywhere to keep his breastplate anchored and steady, he risked leaving his chest uncovered, exposed to the fire-lit arrows of the enemy. The belt, in other words, was the hanger—necessary to organize, secure, and stabilize the rest.

Let's jump ahead here to consider each of the other pieces of armor, focusing on their spiritual description or virtue. This will help us see how truth really is the stabilizer for all of them.

- **RIGHTEOUSNESS** (v. 14) means right living, the process by which we apply truth to our lives and produce conduct honoring and pleasing to God.

- **PEACE** (v. 15) is the deep, inner, eternal stability the believers possess by virtue of their relationship with Jesus, a stability that's not subject to external circumstances. It's also the quality that enables us to live harmoniously with others.
- **FAITH** (v. 16) is the application of what one believes, the process of putting feet to God's truth and living in the light of it, in practical terms.
- **SALVATION** (v. 17) is both our eternal security with Christ, as well as the full inheritance we've been given through relationship with Him. It includes our blessings, status, and identity—everything we've received that enables us to live victoriously for Him.
- **THE WORD OF GOD** (v. 17) is His present, relevant, personal Word to us for today. The Bible may be an old book, but God's Spirit makes it fresh, new, and alive for us each day.
- **PRAYER** (v. 18) is not only the way in which we communicate with God, but also the divinely authorized method by which we grab hold of Christ and gain access to His promises, power, and victory.

OK, now it's your turn. Using all this information, fill in the chart below by describing how the belt of truth is the "hanger" for each one.

Righteousness	The TRUTH is God's Spirit lives in me. Because of this, I can live in a way that is honoring to God.
Peace	
Faith	
Salvation	
The Word of God	
Prayer	

What good can a soldier be in battle if he's not operating hands-free? There's too much to be done. Too many enemy attacks to defend against. Without the ability to move quickly, freely, and nimbly, there's no viable response to the advances of the devil and his demons. But with truth on board, positioned where it belongs, these hands are ready to fight!

Good thing the truth is on our side.

Interestingly, the soldier's belt not only stabilized the other pieces of armor, but it also bore some of the weight, relieving pressure from the shoulders. Without it, the soldier was forced to bear the full weight of everything—most notably the cumbersome breastplate, which otherwise would wear down his energy, making him far less effective in battle.

See the spiritual connection? Without the belt of truth, you're left with the burdensome responsibility of carrying the full weight of your own "breastplate"—your own "righteousness." Instead of God fulfilling your requirement for righteousness, you're on the hook for it. Instead of God making you acceptable in His sight through the sacrifice of His Son, you're responsible for somehow proving yourself spotless and perfect in His sight. Good luck with that, huh? But with God's truth strapped around your body, you're relieved of that pressure. God's Word—truth—reveals that righteousness has been given to you through faith in Christ as a free gift, freeing you from living with the weight of all that sin on your shoulders.

We've considered how truth acts as a "hanger," but in what other ways do you also think truth helps us bear some of the weight and responsibilities of the other spiritual virtues? Explain.

FREEDOM OF MOVEMENT

Ephesians 6 is the only place in Scripture where "girding" is mentioned within a military context. Girding was the act of gathering up a lengthy, draping tunic and tucking it into the girdle to allow free range of motion for the legs. "It is generally agreed that military tunics differed from civilian versions in that they were actually longer."[3] But both types of individuals could be seen wearing one.

Elsewhere in the Scriptures, girding refers generally to a Jewish man who would pull up his traditionally long, draping toga whenever he was about to engage in a task or activity that required him to be more mobile or active. As with the soldier, the purpose of all this girding was to get moving and avoid falling—to experience freedom of movement. Restricting the tunic released and freed the feet.

The weight of a soldier's full service marching armor (including his food rations) was around 66 lbs.[2]

Write John 8:32 below, word for word.

Thinking about 1) the verse you just wrote, 2) what you've learned about truth throughout this week, and 3) the highlighted sentences in the previous paragraph—what kind of relationship do you see between these three? How would you summarize what these tell you?

While this was probably not Paul's direct meaning when writing about girding your loins, the culture and context of this action provides us with a striking illustration and spiritual lesson. Often, when God wants to move you forward to the next level with Him, He may require you to "tuck in your tunic"—to restrict certain things within the boundaries set by His truth. When you willingly submit, true freedom awaits you. You cannot advance against the enemy successfully and keep from tumbling into error unless you are willing to submit to God's truth.

Without truth—without an absolute, nonnegotiable standard—there's no real liberty. Without guidelines that are central and authoritative to our experience, everyone is governed by their own self-regulated principles, which could be faulty or even dangerous to others.

Here's an example: If you live in America, you possess certain inalienable rights that are yours merely by virtue of your citizenship. But just because this nation is "free" does not mean you're free to do whatever you want. There are boundaries, laws, within which everyone must restrict their freedom. Without these boundaries, everyone's personal definition of *freedom* could infringe on others' personal freedoms. So the laws do restrict us, yes, but they also free us to live peaceably and at ease with one another.

Record the details of a time when your allegiance to the truth of God— which perhaps felt restrictive to you at first—actually helped you experience more freedom as a result?

How is aligning yourself with truth different from legalism? Why does legalism confine, yet truth sets you free? (Tough question, I know, but give it some thought and prepare to discuss with your group.)

What are some other things in your life—even good things—that need to be "tucked away" for now to keep you moving forward to the next level with God?

The belt of truth. The clothes hanger for your entire outfit of spiritual weaponry. The safe spot for tucking away those things that often tangle up around your feet and hinder your freedom of movement. As much as we may not like how this girdle pinches and hugs us sometimes, it is meant to reveal a whole new world of opportunity for us. It helps us hold off our enemy and hold a steady course. Truth sets us free.

Actionable Intel...

Legalism is "the act of putting law above gospel by establishing requirements for salvation beyond repentance and faith in Jesus Christ. Legalism reduces the broad, inclusive and general precepts of the Bible to narrow and rigid codes.[4]

DAY 4

WALK THIS WAY

The thing about deception is that it's, well ... deceptive. If it'd just come out as the bold-faced lie it is, we could much more easily detect it and deal with it. But deception is rarely outright. It's a lie cloaked in a tweaked version of truth. A fraud. An illusion. It doesn't announce its arrival or pronounce its intentions. Just lures us toward its sneaky, outstretched fingers until ... Gotcha!

All the more reason why girding ourselves with truth is so imperative. We need something guaranteed to lift the guise of deception and reveal the slick-selling underside. We need a way to expose the one who "disguises himself as an angel of light" (2 Cor. 11:14).

What perspectives or activities have you recently seen in the news or on social media that seemed right but when compared with Scripture, they fell short?

THE BRIGHT LIGHT

As you'll recall, Paul had already discussed each piece of armor described in Ephesians 6 earlier in the letter, including (of course) the importance of truth. Likening it to a belt here was just another way of reiterating what he'd already explained.

*But all things
become visible
when they are
exposed by the light,
for everything that
becomes visible is
light (Eph. 5:13).*

Look at Ephesians 5:13 in the margin. What term correlates to truth in this verse?

What are some of the similarities and connections between the results of truth and light?

When my husband and I travel, we're always required (like everybody) to go through the security post at the airport. The TSA clerks take our driver's licenses and carefully scans our faces to make sure we're who our documents say we are. But they don't stop there. They always hold our licenses under some sort of light scanner to check for authenticity. No matter how many times they've done it to us Shirers before, and no matter how many hundreds of IDs they've examined in their career, they still don't trust their own perception. They always put the ID under that light to be sure the one in their hand at that moment is the real deal, not a fake.

The light is what separates fact from fiction.

If the TSA screeners are that militant about checking for deception, what about us? We must always expose our thoughts and motivations to the light, checking for any bits of deception trying to sneak on board from within.

Our deceiver operates in the darkness. And he hopes we will, too. As long as we're stumbling around shrouded in darkness—not really sure what's true and what's not—we'll never be able to see him for who he really is and detect the underlying intentions of his plans. What we need is a spotlight that pierces the darkness and lays bare all his evil schemes, systems, and illusions. The truth of God's Word is that light!

Satan is the master illusionist. He pulls the wool over our eyes, causing us to think happiness exists where it doesn't, that security is offered where it isn't. He makes evil appealing and righteousness boring, then entices us down a dark path that leaves us addicted, joyless, and empty. It's why we can be convinced that sin isn't sin or that God's way isn't the best way. Somehow the enemy's created the illusion in our minds that these situations are the exception to the rule.

What are the most prevalent cultural philosophies or ideas you've seen teens or adults fall victim to recently?

How can you clearly see the enemy's strategy behind these philosophies or trends?

> *For once you were full of darkness, but now you have light from the Lord. So live as people of light! (Eph. 5:8, NLT).*

Note the various translations in Scripture of some of the Hebrew and Greek terms that unveil the enemy's strategy: illusion, deception, to deceive, delusion, empty, worthless, fantasy.

THE THING ABOUT FEELINGS

Why light? Why truth? It's because nothing else in our lives is steady enough to do what only light and truth can.

Feelings, for example. Feelings change. Emotions are unstable. The right movie with the right music and somber storyline can bring tears to my eyes and threaten to sadden me for the rest of the day. But then, just as abruptly, one of my boys will say or do something cute and put a huge smile back on my face. Why? Because feelings change based on external stimuli.

The same is true of intelligence. Even the most brilliant among us have changed our minds on an issue after acquiring more information or gaining a new perspective. Why? Because minds change.

What about your gut? Every human being has a conscience—that deep, internal instinct that steers you morally. But our conscience is part of our humanity—frail and susceptible to sin, significantly shaped by things like our environment, our parents, our teachers, our life circumstances. Yes, the Holy Spirit awakens and engages our conscience after we're born again, but it's still unreliable as an ultimate source of figuring out truth. Why? Because even the conscience can change.

I'm not suggesting that feelings, intelligence, and instinct can never help you in making life decisions. I'm simply saying that ultimately nothing should be trusted to govern your life like an unchangeable standard.

On a scale of 1 to 10, rate yourself in each area. How much do you tend to depend on any of these factors for guidance when making a life decision:

Feelings

1	2	3	4	5	6	7	8	9	10

Intelligence

1	2	3	4	5	6	7	8	9	10

Instinct

1	2	3	4	5	6	7	8	9	10

Past experiences

| 1 | 2 | 3 | 4 | 5 | 6 | 7 | 8 | 9 | 10 |

When these tools have proven helpful in guiding your decisions, did you use anything else to corroborate them? If so, what? Or whom?

Turn to Numbers 20:7-12. Read it thoroughly, then meet me back here to answer a few questions.

1. What was the Lord's instruction?

2. What portion of the instruction did Moses follow?

3. What did he choose not to obey?

4. Based on Exodus 17:5-6, what might have been Moses' rationale for making this decision?

5. What were the horrible consequences of Moses' actions?

Moses' decision cost him God's most choice blessing. He wouldn't be able to experience the abundance of the promised land because he relied on his own understanding, his feelings, his past experiences—whatever it was—instead of just following God's instructions.

None of these things is an accurate compass of God's truth. Each of them is tainted by our evil environment and is still in the process of being sanctified by the Holy Spirit. They will never be perfect guides, not as long as we live on this planet in these fleshly bodies. No one knows it like our enemy knows it. It's why he cloaks his deceptions in a way that awakens our emotions, excites our instincts, or brings to mind a past experience—all in an attempt to compel us to move forward without consulting truth, veering us off course and outside of God's will.

Again, reason enough why we always need the ever-bright spotlight of God's truth—guiding, directing, regulating everything that comes our way. Our job as belt-of-truth-wearing believers is to recalibrate our feelings, instinct, conscience, and experience to line up with it.

LIVING UNDER THE LIGHT

Yesterday, we took a brief look at John 8:32, in which Jesus said to the believing Jews: "You will know the truth, and the truth will set you free." But equally important is the verse directly preceding it:

Read it carefully:

> *"Then Jesus said to the Jews who had believed him, 'If you continue in my word, you really are my disciples.'" (John 8:31)*

Look at a few other translations of this verse, and then write down what you consider to be Jesus' main point in this statement.

"… if you abide in my word …" (NKJV)

"… if you hold to my teaching …" (NIV)

"… if you remain faithful to my teachings …" (NLT)

"… if you hold fast to my teachings and live in accordance with them …" (AMP)

When Jesus said knowing the truth will "set you free," He wasn't referring to an accumulation of knowledge. Excessive or accurate information has never set anyone free. Knowing things about God doesn't equal honoring Him (Rom. 1:21). In fact, it's quite possible to be very smart and yet become "fools" (Rom. 1:22). Freedom comes to us when we unapologetically follow the truth we discover in Him and in His Word. Walking in it, abiding in it, ordering our steps and decisions according to it—that's what makes the difference. That's what disarms the enemy's influence and his impact in our lives.

As you gather your intel from this last day of study, ask yourself: "Have I made a commitment to God's truth as the guiding directive for my life?" and "What is God asking me to do as a result of the truth I know?" Carefully consider any areas of your life where you are allowing your feelings, gut instincts, or previous experiences to be the determining factor for your actions, then realign your allegiance to the "Light of life." Ask the Lord to give you the courage to hold up His Word as a banner over your life. And as you do—as He does—"your ears will hear a voice behind you, saying, 'This is the way; walk in it'" (Isa. 30:21, NIV).

Actionable Intel...

Then Jesus again spoke to them, saying, "I am the Light of the world; he who follows Me will not walk in the darkness, but will have the Light of life" (John 8:12).

DAY 5
STRATEGY SESSION

When Roman soldiers were being disciplined for inappropriate behavior, a superior officer would often punish them by "making them stand outside headquarters clad only in their tunics and without their belts so that they looked rather ridiculous in long tunics and deprived of the one item that marked them as soldiers."[6] To be caught without their belts was embarrassing to them. Punishment.

The belt, after all, marked them as soldiers.

You are a soldier in the Lord's army. You should constantly and consistently be marked by the truth of your God. And it should be an embarrassment—a shocking word to use perhaps, but let's go with it— an embarrassment to be caught without it.

God's truth should be a banner that flies high on the flagpole of your life and over those you love and share relationship with. The church, as His body and warrior against darkness in the culture, should be known for its commitment to the unchanging, absolute truth of our great God. Without this prevailing standard, we'll always be subject to falling for the enemy's dangling carrots.

Truth. Don't leave home without it.

As you prepare to craft your strategy for today, take a brief moment to consider one more thing with me. The Genesis account of Adam and Eve is one of the most familiar in Scripture. You may be tempted not to look too closely at it right now, seeing as you've read it dozens, maybe hundreds of times. But I urge you to take the time to do it anyway. The Holy Spirit has a knack for making old stories fresh and new, brimming with renewed insight into Him and into your own heart.

Turn to Genesis 2:16-17, as well as 3:1-6. Read both passages carefully.

1. What was the truth—the standard set by God?

2. What did the enemy say to Eve to slant the truth?

3. What do you think made the enemy's proposal so appealing?

4. What was the ripple effect of the enemy's deception?

Now personalize this story. What are the unique ways the enemy makes his way appealing to you? Explain.

The tempter's falsehood in the garden of Eden was so clever and sounded so decadent to the first couple that Satan was able to persuade them to rebel against God, destroying perfection not only for themselves but for all their descendants—for all of us. Those are pretty high stakes. Must've been a pretty strong delusion. Even in a perfect setting, with perfectly intact identities, in perfect relationship with the Father, they allowed the enemy to lead them down a path containing devastating generational consequences. He drew Eve's attention to what she couldn't have, tricking her into ignoring all the abundance God told her she could have.

Satan's strategy against you is equally clever. He plans to zero in on your deepest insecurities and desires with the intention of showing you how you can bypass God to meet every single one. But we're not falling for it anymore, are we? The spotlight of God's truth is going to expose every single scheme of the enemy.

With the prayer strategy you're about to craft—and the belt of truth you're going to wear—you can be girded and protected from this day forward. So, open up your journal and get started.

THE DIVINE WARRIOR

New Testament interpretation commonly leans on Old Testament passages as the foundation of authority. The apostle Paul's description of the armor most certainly does. It reverberates with deliberately chosen language to connect it with the Book of Isaiah. Ephesians 6 alludes to the image of Yahweh depicted as a Divine Warrior.

> *"Truth is missing, and whoever turns from evil is plundered. The LORD saw that there was no justice, and he was offended. He saw that there was no man—he was amazed that there was no one interceding; so his own arm brought salvation, and his own righteousness supported him. He put on righteousness as body armor, and a helmet of salvation on his head; he put on garments of vengeance for clothing, and he wrapped himself in zeal as in a cloak. So he will repay according to their deeds: fury to his enemies, retribution to his foes, and he will repay the coasts and islands. They will fear the name of the LORD in the west and his glory in the east; for he will come like a rushing stream driven by the wind of the LORD"* (Isa. 59:15–19).

The context of warfare was clearly evident in the Isaianic passage. The nation of Israel—God's people as a whole—was corrupt and its leaders debased. The pure worship of Yahweh had been replaced by unapologetic idolatry and perverted cultic practices like sorcery, prostitution, and child sacrifice. In response to this demoralization, God Himself responds by donning His armor, in essence His own character and virtues, to bring judgment and justice. And, sadly, the enemy is not some other pagan nation. In this case, it is the children of God themselves.

This warfare tone provides the backdrop for Ephesians. Except now, the good news of the gospel severely changes the dynamics. Under the new covenant established in Christ, the hostility and enmity between the Father and humanity has been dissolved. Now, that which Yahweh was once compelled to use against His people, He freely gives as a gift to them—to exact against the devil and the domain of darkness. With Christ as the cornerstone, the church is fitted together and equipped to advance as one body. One unit. A divine warrior. The church is the presence of God on earth through which He continues to wage warfare and claim the victory that has already been secured in His beloved Son.

Please do not miss the beautiful and stunning implications: your armor is Yahweh's own armor—given as a gift and empowered by His Spirit to ensure victory.

THE BREASTPLATE OF
RIGHTEOUSNESS

Think about the word invitation. Who are some people you'd like to receive an invitation from? What are some activities you'd love to be invited to do?

Now, think about your home. In the last few months, who have you invited into your home? Why did you ask that person to visit your house?

When you invite someone into your home, it's usually because you know that person well or want to get to know them better. We don't often invite complete strangers whose intentions are unclear into our homes. That's why people like plumbers and electricians often have to undergo background checks and repair companies are bonded and insured. To invite someone into our homes is to give them access to the things that are most important to us.

Unrighteousness is what gives the enemy an invitation to make himself at home in our lives. He feels welcome into your experience when you choose to live in ways that are not God's standard. When you don't line your choices, behaviors, and actions up with the Scriptures, you don't have the opportunity to truly deflect the enemy's advances in your life. To live unrighteously is to allow the devil to have a foothold in your life.

Look over Ephesians 6:10-19 again. List the first three pieces of armor below.

1.

2.

3.

Now, list the last three.

4.

5.

6.

Look over these two lists. Can you detect how the first list of pieces of armor is different from the second? Discuss.

Look carefully and you'll notice that the first three pieces are described like a uniform that we should *put on* and wear daily: the belt of truth, the breastplate of righteousness, and making sure our feet are shod with the gospel of peace. It is truth, righteousness, and peace that allow us to stand against the schemes of the devil.

The final three are the tools we take up in the heat of battle, in the exact moment we need them. Think about baseball or softball players who wear uniforms no matter where they are stationed on the field—and even in the dugout. They keep their bat and helmet on hand and ready at a moment's notice. Then, when it's her turn at the plate, she trades her soft cap for the sturdy helmet, picks up the bat and heads out to the field. Through it all, the uniform remains on.

Read Ephesians 6:14. What part of the uniform does Paul call our attention to at the end of verse 14?

As Christians, a key part of our uniform and defense against the attacks of the enemy is right living—righteousness. Every single day, we are to make choices that align with God's expectations. That's actually the definition of righteousness: upright living that aligns with the expectations of God.

Underline the definition of righteousness in the paragraph above. How might truly understanding that definition and living it out change our behaviors? Attitudes? The way we treat others? The way we think about ourselves?

Remember we learned last week that those who gird themselves with truth choose a lifestyle that affirms God's standard. This means to uphold it, support it, pledge our allegiance to it as our standard. Doing this is the sturdy foundation upon which righteousness is built. You can't live right if you don't have the right standard to govern your behavior. It is only after you have put on the belt that you can live in a way that aligns with God's standard.

The truth is like the train tracks and your righteousness is the train. The devil's goal is to derail your train of behavior and righteous living off the tracks of God's truth. He celebrates, encourages, and tempts you toward unrighteous living every single time he has an opportunity. Do you think it's coincidence that a particular temptation happens to come to you in those moments when you are particularly weak, or lonely, or exhausted?

Our God does not tempt us, but the enemy does. When is he most often to pounce on you? When you're tired? Lonely? Frustrated? Some other time?

Considering all you've learned about the devil so far in our study, why do you think he picks these moments of weakness to tempt us toward unrighteousness?

We're the ones who make the choice to pursue sin. But the enemy is going to try to catch you at your weakest moments in order to make it more enticing. He is strategic. He wants to know what your weaknesses are and where you've misstepped in the past. He is marking all of that so he can come up with the exact temptation he hopes will lead you down a path of unrighteousness. And here's why: unrighteousness leaves us open to a full, frontal attack by the enemy.

That's why we can't just affirm God's truth; we must also align our lives to it. In other words, you can read all of the stuff about how great our God is, and who He has made us to be, and the value He's placed on our lives, and the great riches that are available to us in Jesus Christ. We can read all of that. And Amen all that, and wave our hands at church on Sunday and sing hymns about it, and get on our knees and pray about it. But unless we're willing to actually do it, to live in alignment with it ... that's what the breastplate is. The breastplate is aligning your life to God's expectations and standard.

Read Romans 7:15-20 aloud. What do these verses—also written by Paul— teach us about the reality of choosing to align our lives with God's standard?

Living according to God's standard isn't easy. If we aren't careful and don't rely on God's spirit to empower us, we—like the Apostle Paul—can become easily overwhelmed. If God's standard is complete holiness and obedience, that's unattainable, right?

That realization can leave us discouraged or seeking to perform for God, trying to attain perfection in our own strength. The good news is we don't have to.

Turn to the inside back cover and look at the drawing of the Roman soldier's armor. How do the belt and the breastplate work together?

The belt carries the weight of the breastplate, taking it from the soldier's shoulders and freeing him to fight the battle. In our lives, the Belt of Truth carries the weight of our pursuit of righteousness.

Read the following verses aloud: Philippians 3:9, Romans 5:19, 1 Peter 2:24, and 2 Corinthians 5:21. What do these verses have in common?

The good news is the perfect One has already come. We don't have to pay the wages of our sin because Jesus Christ lovingly, graciously, generously, and lavishly paid the price for your sin and mine. And when He did, He didn't just leave us empty. He credited us with all of His perfection, righteousness, and holiness.

This means that no matter where you've been, no matter where I've been, thank God, no matter what we've done, no matter the bad choices that we've made, no matter our past, no matter the relationships, no matter the hiccups along the way, still you and I are the righteousness of God in Christ Jesus. And that truth helps take some of the weight off your shoulders.

Now, read Ephesians 1:13-14. What other gift have we been given as believers?

How does the Holy Spirit help us to live according to God's standard?

This Holy Spirit gives us the power to do what we cannot in our own strength. It is the Holy Spirit's job to make us more like Jesus. Righteousness, then, is not behavior management, but change that comes from the inside out as the Holy Spirit chips away everything in our lives that does not look like Jesus—including attitudes, friends, habits, and actions.

Read 2 Thessalonians 2:13. What is the Holy Spirit's job, according to this verse?

The Holy Spirit's job is to sanctify us. Sanctification is the process by which you are molded into the image of Christ Jesus. It is the process by which you are conformed into the image of Christ. And it is not your major responsibility to bear. It is the responsibility, the job description, of the Holy Spirit.

Think about the Roman soldier's armor once again. What do you think the breastplate's primary role was?

The breastplate protected the most vital organs of the soldier, most notably the heart. Your heart is the centerpiece of your soul, so it's no wonder the enemy is after your heart. If he can get you in your heart, your core, he's got you in the palm of his hand. Live Proverbs 4:23 this week: Guard your heart!

DAY 1
THE HEART OF THE MATTER

The heart. Arguably the most vital organ in your whole body.

Right now, your heart is beating in your chest, dispersing blood through your veins and arteries, picking up oxygen and other nutrients and supplying them to places where they can be turned into raw energy. That's why a feeble or malfunctioning heart creates such a noticeable ripple effect throughout a person's entire system. Without the heart's continuous pumping action, the body feels the diminishing effects, until ultimately, it ceases to function altogether.

So your heart is the seat of your life. The source. And what the physical heart is to your physical life, the spiritual heart is to your spiritual life.

Using the previous paragraph as your guide, how would you describe the vital actions the spiritual heart contributes to your spiritual life?

What does Proverbs 4:23 in the margin command us, regarding the heart?

Why do you think this is necessary? Explain.

> *Guard your heart above all else, for it is the source of life (Prov. 4:23, CSB).*

GUARD YOUR HEART

Once a Roman soldier was fitted with his belt (the subject of last week's study), he would put on his breastplate. The breastplate was a metal shield (usually bronze), worn over the midsection from the neck to the thighs. During Paul's era, the typical Roman legionary wore this protective piece of equipment (called the *thoraka*) over a leather sheath-like garment. And if he was wealthy enough to afford it, he would also don a coat of mail over his breastplate for extra fortification.

The purpose of all these layers was to guard the vital organs, particularly the heart. In case of a direct hit to the soldier's upper body, wearing

The Greek word for breastplate is thoraka, *since it was designed to guard the thorax— a term meaning the trunk or chest.*[1]

"Mail armor was made of iron rings about 7 millimeters in diameter, stitched onto a backing."[2]

the breastplate could mean the difference between life and death. One swift strike from an enemy sword could stop a man's heartbeat cold.

Turn to the image of a Roman soldier on the inside back cover. Use Ephesians 6:14 to fill in the spiritual virtue Paul connected to the breastplate.

Write your own definition of this virtue below.

Why do you think wearing the belt of truth is a necessary prerequisite for wearing the breastplate of righteousness?

Righteousness literally means *justice*—the quality of being upright, fulfilling the expectations set in a relationship. In our case as believers, this relationship is with God Himself. Righteousness, then, is upright living that aligns with God's expectations.

Rewrite the last line of the previous paragraph in your own words.

This definition is similar to what we studied last week, when looking at truth, but there's a unique nuance that makes righteousness the more practical of the two. While the lifestyle of a person girded in the belt of truth affirms God's standard, someone who puts on the breastplate of righteousness aligns his or her life to it. Truth provides the grid; righteousness paints the picture. Righteousness is right living— walking "in a manner worthy of the calling to which you have been called" (Eph. 4:1, ESV).

Describe the subtle difference between truth and righteousness.

How do you think "right living" can act as a guard against the enemy's attacks in your life? Explain.

Last year, before my family and I went on a long ministry trip, I cleared the refrigerator and pantry of any food that might spoil while we were away. But in all the busyness and chaos of cleaning and packing for five, I completely overlooked the bowl of fruit we keep in the middle of our kitchen table. The bananas and apples were already at the point where they needed to be eaten quickly before they went bad. But I left them right there. For ten days.

So you can imagine the friends they'd made by the time we got home. Fruit flies were buzzing everywhere, in nearly every nook and cranny. They mobbed us just about anywhere we tried to sit or stand in that part of the house. And we swatted, snorted, shooed, and slapped at them until we all wanted to scream.

I don't know if you've ever tried getting rid of these critters, but prepare for an arduous, exhausting task. I found a myriad of solutions on Pinterest (and tried every single one!), but just when we thought they might be gone, there were more. And then more. They'd either arrived in droves from the start, or they made a lot of babies while they were there.

But here's the point: I didn't need to personally invite them into my house. All I had to do was create an environment conducive for them, and they just invited themselves. The environment I created WAS the invitation.

The enemy takes every opportunity to push his way into our lives. And unrighteousness is all the invitation he needs to send his demons on assignment. It not only leaves the door open, but also rolls out a welcome mat on the doorstep of your soul! It actually attracts enemy intrusion in our lives, allowing him to make himself at home. The "one who knows the right thing to do and does not do it" sins (Jas. 4:17), and sin exposes you to Satan's jabs.

And the heart is one of his primary and lethal targets.

In your own life, or in the life of someone you love, when have you seen wrong choices and behavior become a "welcome mat" for demonic activity to infiltrate?

HEART AND SOUL

Most of us probably have our own idea of what the Bible means when it refers to our heart, but let's drill down a little bit to refine that idea. Human beings are made up of three distinct parts: 1) body, which allows you to relate to the physical world; 2) spirit, which allows you to relate to God; and 3) soul, which allows you to relate to yourself. Your soul is what makes you a unique individual. It's your personality, your distinctive internal nature, and it is composed of four factors:

- mind (your thoughts)
- will (your ambition)
- emotion (your feelings)
- conscience (your moral compass)

When Scripture speaks of your heart, it's referring to the intersection of these four internal characteristics. The heart is the centerpiece of the soul.

Given the four parts of the soul, why do you think this would be a primary target of the devil?

Watch the enemy at work on all four levels:

- **Your Mind:** Distorting your thinking with lies about God, His Word, and even yourself, trying to cripple your soul through negative, unbiblical thought processes.

- **Your Will:** Redirecting your ambitions away from eternal, godly pursuits and luring you toward interests that are temporal, short-sighted, and even directly opposed to the will of God.

- **Your Emotions:** Tampering with your feelings, piggybacking on runaway responses like anger, discouragement, revenge, or sadness to persuade you into making unstable choices.

- **Your Conscience:** Influencing your conscience so it steers you to live in a way that doesn't line up with biblical guidelines.

When you and I choose not to align our actions with God's truth—when we live in blatant rebellion against His will for us—we leave our heart exposed where Satan can take a clear shot.

Try personalizing this teaching for yourself. How have you recognized the enemy targeting your …

- **Thinking?**

- **Ambitions?**

- **Feelings?**

- **Conscience?**

Wearing the belt of truth, putting on the shoes and helmet, using the shield or sword—they'll do you no good if you leave your heart open to a full frontal attack by the devil. You must intentionally protect the organ that pumps vibrancy into your spiritual life. So pray fervently. Seek God fully. Ask Him to reveal anything "spoiled" in your life that's attracting the pesky fruit flies of demonic activity. Then confess it and repent of it, defusing the accusations of the enemy.

But no matter what the current state of your soul, and no matter how far you might currently be from a lifestyle of righteousness, don't be discouraged. A sudden infusion of righteousness can change the whole environment, sometimes in a hurry (see Ps. 81:13–14).

So let's clean house and guard our hearts starting today.

Actionable Intel...

DAY 2
THE CLEAN SWEEP

What the breastplate did for the Roman soldier's physical heart, righteousness does for your spiritual heart. Guards it. Protects it. Shields it from your enemy's attempts to exact fatal blows to this life-giving source in your soul. But understanding how to use this piece of spiritual armor requires you to truly understand what righteousness is and how it works.

THE MANY FACES OF RIGHTEOUSNESS

The concept of righteousness is mentioned many times in Scripture, in several different capacities, and I want us to look at them together. We're going to wade into some theological waters over the next couple days, but don't get overwhelmed. Just stick with me for a bit, and it'll all make sense. So lean in and listen for God's voice as you study.

Here we go.

1. PERFECT RIGHTEOUSNESS

God is perfect—as is His standard of righteousness. When we look at this type of righteousness, it seems that wearing the breastplate is an absolute impossibility. If left to our own devices, there is no way we can meet this standard. As a mere human being with the spiritual DNA of Adam and Eve coursing through our bodies, we are not—I repeat: NOT—righteous. "All have sinned and fall short of the glory of God" (Rom. 3:23). Even the most good-natured among us, on our very best day, fall woefully shy of God's expectations.

Read Romans 3:10-12 and Isaiah 64:6. What is the main principle of these two passages?

If God's perfection is what Paul was referring to when he commanded us to put on the breastplate of righteousness, we'd all be in big trouble. Perfection is an utterly impossible, utterly unreasonable quest. (Trust me, I've tried it.) And the enemy would even like to use this to his advantage, inciting us to chase perfectionism instead of chasing God. If we aren't careful, this pursuit can become a bottomless pit of idolatry. He'll promptly fit us with shackles that will leave us in a state of total exhaustion while we're working like crazy to prove ourselves fit for heaven. All the while, the breastplate that protects us against Satan goes unused and unworn. Ironically enough, we can be just as bound by the pursuit of perfection as by any addiction to alcohol or pornography.

Do you tend to struggle with perfectionism? If so, how does it impact your life? Explain.

In what ways, if any, is your perfectionism rooted in a desire to seek God's approval? What about a desire to receive approval or commendation from other people?

Read 1 Kings 12:25-33 for a biblical example of someone seeking to adjust God's standards to suit his personal goals and convenience.

Since God's perfect righteousness is an unattainable goal for us to reach on our own, what's the solution? How do we shake free from our legalistic do-gooding, while at the same time meeting God's standard and wearing the breastplate that keeps us protected from demonic assault? Well, we could lower or <u>modify God's standard,</u> couldn't we? We often want Him to be like the teacher who grades on the curve, lowering the requirements for a passing grade. We think He should be willing to adjust His standard to suit us. Cut us some slack. Bring His expectations down to our level, calling our lifestyle "righteous" when it's really just a modified, watered-down version of His righteousness.

For not knowing about God's righteousness and seeking to establish their own, they did not subject themselves to the righteousness of God (Rom. 10:3).

Look at Romans 10:3 in the margin. *Underline* **the portion of the verse that describes what Paul said these people were trying to do.** *Circle* **what he said they didn't do. Record some specific ways you've noticed people "seeking to establish" their own standard of righteousness.**

Is there any way that you have knowingly or inadvertently adjusted God's standards throughout your life to fit your personal preferences or traditions? Are there any ways you might be doing it now?

2. COMPARATIVE RIGHTEOUSNESS

OK, so maybe perfectionism is not where you get hung up. But what about this? In 1 Samuel 24, the saga of Saul and David's strained relationship hit a climactic moment. King Saul, jealously outraged by David's popularity among the people, had set out to kill his perceived rival. And David, along with his little ragtag band of fighting men, had holed up in a cave to steer clear of danger. But a precarious circumstance arose when Saul stepped into the same cave to (ahem) "relieve himself" (v. 3), completely unaware that David was sitting in the dark recesses of the cave, watching his every move.

Saul was right there. In a completely vulnerable position. David could've crept from the shadows and brought this whole chase scene to a final, bloody end. But instead, he inched out of the darkness and merely "cut off the edge of Saul's robe secretly" (v. 4). Not until Saul had finished his business, left the cave, and walked a safe distance away did David come out, call to the king, bow low to the ground before him, and then hold out the piece of torn cloth as proof that he could've hurt Saul, but didn't.

Read 1 Samuel 24:16-17 to see what happened next.
What was Saul's emotional response to what David had done (v. 16)?

How did Saul measure his own level of righteousness (v. 17)?

Comparison is an often-used method for determining one's righteousness. But comparison is never an accurate barometer, because righteousness is adherence to God's perfect standard. So even if your actions are better than someone else's, they're still not as good as God's.

Comparison soothes but it also deceives, making us feel justified with sinful actions. It can be disheartening when we see others doing better than us. Either way, it's inaccurate—which is why the devil loves it. He works to keep us looking at others instead of looking at God Himself.

Be honest here. Who are the people—friends or even strangers— whom you tend to compare yourself to? Why?

How does it make you feel when you measure yourself as better than them? Circle some adjectives.

superior • justified • proud • accomplished • mature • smart • confident

How does it make you feel to think you are worse than them?

depressed • inferior • weak • ignorant • resigned • embarrassed • regretful

God's perfect righteousness can be discouraging because we have no hope of reaching it on our own. And comparative righteousness is deceiving because it's a measurement against an inaccurate standard. So neither of these options can be the breastplate that Paul is referring to. There must be another way—a way to be truly righteous. Without being perfect. Without just trying to be better than everybody else.

Thankfully, there is.

This third option will help lead the way.

3. IMPUTED RIGHTEOUSNESS

The cross took away the penalty of our sin. It doesn't just mean He's declared it a wash. ("All that sin of yours? We'll just forget about all that, OK?") No. Your sin and mine required a just payment. Death. For all of it. And Jesus paid it. Death. For all of it. For all who would receive Him by faith.

And honestly, if that's the sum total of what the cross accomplished for us—escaping what we deserve: eternal separation from God in hell— this fact alone should be enough to garner our unending gratitude, causing us to fall on our knees in awed worship every single day.

But the cross really is the gift that keeps on giving. Because it didn't just take something from us, it gave something miraculous to us.

Open your Bible to Romans 4:22-24 and meditate on these verses in light of Genesis 15:6 in the margin. What action did Abraham take?

> **THE CROSS DIDN'T JUST TAKE SOMETHING FROM YOU. IT GAVE SOMETHING MIRACULOUS TO YOU.**
> *#ArmorOfGodStudy*

> *Abram believed the LORD, and He credited it to him as righteousness (Gen. 15:6, CSB).*

What was God's response?

Why was Abraham's story mentioned again in the New Testament?

To whom does this promise apply?

When you trust Jesus as your personal Savior, the penalty of sin is removed and the gift of God's own righteousness is given (imputed) to you. It is "credited" to your spiritual account. The perfection and holiness of God Himself has become yours in Christ.

So when God looks at you now, He no longer sees your humanity, your frailty, your sin ... your unrighteousness. He sees you through the blood-stained filter of His own Son, the perfect Lamb of God. You no longer need to exhaust yourself striving for perfection. You are already completely, wholly, and perfectly righteous because of Christ's gift to you.

Perfect righteousness discourages you.

Comparative righteousness deceives you.

Imputed righteousness defines you and declares you innocent before all accusers.

Listen to me closely now. The enemy is constantly on the warpath to keep you from realizing and using this gift. He doesn't want you to rest in the fact that your sins have been completely forgiven, that your current status and position is one of complete righteousness before God. He knows as long as you don't see yourself as a righteous, holy child of God, you can never get around to wearing the breastplate that blocks him from successfully attacking the most vital part of your life— your heart. He knows that your knowledge and acceptance of imputed righteousness is the key.

The completeness of pardon for past offense and the integrity of character that belong to the justified life are woven together into an impenetrable [breastplate].[3]
G. G. Findlay

So hear me loud and clear: YOU ARE RIGHTEOUS.

Seriously, say it out loud where the devil can hear you and be assured you're not messin' around:

"I AM RIGHTEOUS!"

Right now as you hold this book in your hands. As you brush your teeth tonight. As you deal with difficult homework. As you struggle to keep your relationships intact. As you wade through troubled emotions. As you fight anxiety or fear or depression. No matter what your present circumstances or past entails. None of the ailments of life can take away what the cross has given you. "The old things passed away; behold, new things have come" (2 Cor. 5:17).

And now, because you know it, you can wear the breastplate because of it.

Actionable Intel...

DAY 3

PERFECT MAKES PRACTICE

I played the piano growing up. And didn't like it. My parents put my sister and me in lessons a couple times a week with Mrs. Roberson, a beautiful yet strict teacher. I loved her, just not the piano. It didn't have enough action for me. Gymnastics? Cheerleading? Track and field? Yes. Sitting still on a wooden bench, however, staring at theory books and running my fingers up and down octaves? Not so much. But I did it anyway, goaded along by the same principle you've probably heard from your own parents or grandparents: Practice makes perfect.

Most of us carry this theme into many areas of our lives. We work long and hard to hone a skill or master a task. We discipline ourselves until our actions and performance are as close to flawless as possible.

But this principle doesn't apply to every situation. And one of the areas where it can actually cause a problem is in our spiritual lives—when we practice and practice in the illusive pursuit of perfection, either to gain approval from God (which is completely unnecessary since we already have it) or simply to impress others. To wear the breastplate of righteousness properly, we need to switch things up a bit.

List the three types of righteousness we discussed in Day 2 and describe each one in your own words.

1.

2.

3.

PUTTING OFF/PUTTING ON

Remember, each of the pieces of spiritual armor Paul employed in Ephesians 6 were mnemonic devices that represented principles he'd already explained. In a series of verses from chapter 4, for example, Paul had introduced a fourth type of righteousness: practical righteousness. And he went to great lengths to explain what it looks and sounds like.

Read Ephesians 4:22-24 in the margin. Underline any key words or phrases that jump out to you in these verses.

> *Put off your old self, which belongs to your former manner of life and is corrupt through deceitful desires, and ... be renewed in the spirit of your minds, and put on the new self, created after the likeness of God in true righteousness and holiness (Eph. 4:22-24, ESV).*

Paul wisely used some key phrases the believers in the Ephesian culture would quickly identify and understand. In their day, part of the initiation process for someone involved in one of their pagan religions was to remove and discard their old clothing, signifying a total break with any previous association. So when Paul implored the Christians to "put off" their old apparel, he wasn't just talking about the routine changing of clothes for the day. He was emphasizing the act of formally rejecting behaviors that were characteristic of their old self, those that aligned with "darkness" instead of "Light" (Eph. 5:8), thereby breaking association with their previous manner of living. This was the next step in living righteously—in practical righteousness—before God.

From the following verses, make a list of behaviors Paul instructed us to put off.

- **Ephesians 4:25**

- **Ephesians 4:26**

- **Ephesians 4:28**

- **Ephesians 4:29**

- **Ephesians 4:31**

- **Ephesians 5:3-5**

Circle any of the attributes in Paul's list that you struggle to put off.

Some of the clothes in my closet—honestly, they're so old and worn, I have no business wearing them any longer, even just around the house. Or their style is so dated, they don't really belong in this century. But I struggle to get rid of them because they fit me so naturally and comfortably. I'm just used to them.

Sometimes lifestyle choices and habits are the same. You may have indulged lust for so long, for example, or lived tethered to pride or anger for so many years that it's become a comfortable outfit for you. But they are symbolic of your old life. Dated. Antiquated. Out of character. Putting it off daily won't be easy, but by God's Spirit it can be done.

Consider the words you circled a minute ago. What comfort or benefit do they give you that makes it difficult for you to part with them?

How have they been harmful to your life? Be specific.

What would be a first step you could take this week to put them off?

"Putting off" was not the end of Paul's instruction. Just because you've gotten undressed doesn't mean you're clothed again. "Putting off" does not automatically equal "putting on." Wearing the breastplate of righteousness means replacing your old garments with carefully selected attributes that align with the light of Christ. This is practical righteousness.

Look back at Ephesians 4:24, then complete this phrase:
Put on the new self … created after the _____.

Use the following verses to compile a list of virtues Paul commanded us to put on.

- **Ephesians 4:2-3**

- **Ephesians 4:25**

- **Ephesians 4:32**

Interestingly, in the pagan religions of ancient Ephesus, it was believed that "the donning of the garment consecrated the initiate so that he or she was filled with the powers of the cosmos and shared in the divine life."[4] Again, just as Paul knew his audience would understand the importance of putting off their old way of life, he knew they'd also understand the analogy of "putting on" new behaviors to align with a new belief system. It wasn't just a change in behavior; they would have understood it as symbolic of an incorporation of power from a new divine order. In this case, from the one true God.

Which of the virtues you listed from Ephesians 4 are the most difficult for you to put on?

What current relationships and circumstances make this most difficult right now?

In Week 1, you wrote down the name of a person or circumstance that is proving difficult to deal with right now. How can you proactively put on these virtues in the next 24 hours in regard to this situation?

Reread and carefully consider the highlighted portion of the last paragraph. Now, using these Scripture references as a guide, draw a line to connect each of the following virtues with the spiritual benefit you can expect to receive and experience if you resolve to put them on.

Humility/meekness (Matt. 5:5)   Enjoy a long, productive life

Wisdom (Prov. 2:1-6)   Prosper

Honoring the Sabbath   Reap eternal harvest
(Isa. 58:13-14)

Honoring parents (Eph. 6:2-3)   Inherit the earth

Obedience (Deut. 28:1-6)   All-around blessing

Delight yourself in the law   Understand the fear of the Lord
of the Lord (Ps. 1:2-3)

Sowing spiritual seed   Delight yourself in the Lord
(Gal. 6:8)

Practical righteousness involves both putting off and putting on. These actions ARE the breastplate of righteousness. Mind if I say that again? We put on the breastplate of righteousness by making a conscious decision and a firm, consistent resolve to "cast off the works of darkness and put on the armor of light" (Rom. 13:12, ESV). Unlike imputed righteousness, it's not a once-in-a-lifetime action. It is a moment-by-moment, day-by-day, repeated choice and action. Again and again. When you choose practical righteousness, you place a blockade between the enemy and the area of your life he most commonly targets—your heart.

Put off. Put on. Practice righteousness.

But I know what you're thinking: *"If only it were that easy."* Right?

How would you describe the difference between imputed righteousness (p. 78) and practical righteousness?

For I do not understand what I am doing, because I do not practice what I want to do, but I do what I hate ... For I do not do the good that I want to do, but I practice the evil that I do not want to do (Rom. 7:15,19, CSB).

See what Jesus thought about this when He addressed the Pharisees in Matthew 23:25-28.

PERFECT. MAKES. PRACTICE.

You're right, of course. Getting our flesh to cooperate with us is a difficult task. Not just for you. For everybody. It feels a lot like the battle Paul described in Romans 7. Look at the verses in the margin, and hear the frustration in Paul's tone of voice. Can you relate to it? I sure can.

Yes, corralling our flesh can be monstrously hard. And even when we do experience some success at modifying our behavior, important internal realities might still be left unaddressed. It's a struggle to address internal sins like lust and pride, or to purify our motivations and energize our attitudes with joy. Have you ever dutifully cleaned your room because your parents told you to, yet did it all with seething anger and distaste for your parents? Yeah, sometimes that's how we obey God on the outside while simmering in disobedience on the inside.

And both of these realities—internal and external—matter to God. Good behavior does not hide a sin-filled heart from God. We are to be righteousness through and through, not just in our behavior. So thankfully, there's real help for us as we seek to put our practical righteousness into practice. And it's firmly rooted in the verse that ties together the various "put off" and "put on" verses in Ephesians 4.

Turn to Ephesians 4:23 and write it word-for-word in the space below.

I know it doesn't often feel this way, but your new self is the righteous nature and very holiness of God (imputed righteousness). That's the real you. At your core, you are pulsing with the new life of Christ. And guess what? "For the fruit of the light consists of all goodness, righteousness, and truth" (Eph 5:9, CSB). He's just amazing that way.

And the way He does it, according to Scripture, is by renewing us in the spirit of our minds. It's what God's Spirit does in us and for us. It's not something you or I can initiate. He does it. God's renewing work within us is what makes our putting off and putting on possible. Practical righteousness is an essential, logical, organic offshoot of imputed righteousness.

So in Ephesians 4, Paul was basically saying, "Righteousness is already *in* you. Now it needs to be *on* you." You must make a conscious choice to act in a way that is consistent with your new life in Christ. And because the Spirit is always there to renew your mind, your potential of producing spiritual fruit is not just potential. It's available. It's doable.

In other words, "Perfect makes practice." Don't get caught up in trying to practice your way to an elusive state of perfection. Instead, flip the script and rely on the perfect nature of Christ in you to affect your practice every single day.

In what ways have you felt exhausted or discouraged lately at the work involved in trying to change or fix yourself?

How does knowing that God's Spirit is the One shouldering this responsibility encourage you and compel you to cooperate with Him?

So if wearing the breastplate—if all this "putting off" and "putting on" is proving particularly difficult lately—realize you're not alone. But realize something else, too: you have an invisible partner every time you jump into battle and tug that breastplate over your heart. God is doing something this very minute to help you do what you otherwise could not. He is renewing your mind, realigning your passions and attitudes, and giving you strength to live in a way that is pleasing to Him and a blessing to others. What a perfect alternative to practice.

Actionable Intel...

DAY 4
PICKLES AND ICE CREAM

When I was pregnant with my second son, I became obsessed with cookies-and-cream SONIC Blasts®. I'd order a small but would ask for it in a medium size cup so there'd be room for extra whipped cream on top. You know, for good measure.

Then one day I had a hankering for something else, something I'd never really wanted before, pregnant or not. I just couldn't get the taste out of my mind. The scent seemed to follow me around like a little lost puppy. The desire to eat a pickle was so strong and palatable in me that I asked my husband to go grab one from the store. Right then. And, oh—if you don't mind, honey, would you please stop by SONIC and get my favorite dessert too?

I don't know if he minded or not. He didn't say as he was going out the door. All I know is I sat in bed that night and gobbled up Oreo-flavored ice cream—and a pickle. Simultaneously. Seems unbelievably strange now, but it sure was delightful at the time. The new life growing inside of me had changed my taste buds, tweaking my passions and desires in new and unexpected ways.

That's just what new life does as it's growing inside you. Blossoming. Maturing.

List the four types of righteousness you've learned in this week of Bible study.

1.

2.

3.

4.

Circle the type that is parallel to the breastplate of righteousness. How is imputed righteousness critical to wearing the breastplate? Explain it in your own words.

Describe the critical work of God's Spirit in our ability to implement practical righteousness in our lives.

What are some specific ways you've noticed your "taste buds" changing in the following areas since becoming a believer—or maybe just lately?

Attitude

Actions

Interests

Desires

Ambitions

Perspectives

WELCOME CHANGE

Changed behaviors, as well as the changed internal attitudes that produce changed behaviors, are each natural outcomes of healthy growth. Babies don't need to work hard to change. They don't even need to concentrate on it. All they need is to be well cared for. And when they are, the natural outcome is growth—which automatically creates change. A baby that isn't changing, isn't growing. And if these things aren't happening, we assume the child is unhealthy.

So if you want to grow in righteousness and see your life transformed from the inside out, spiritual health must be your focus. One of the most cunning tricks of the enemy is to get us to sink our energy into changing instead of focusing it on cultivating health and wellness in Christ. But if we concentrate on having a vibrant, healthy spiritual life, we'll automatically grow and change as a result.

God has chosen you from the beginning for salvation through sanctification by the Spirit and faith in the truth (2 Thess. 2:13b).

According to the last line of 2 Thessalonians 2:13 in the margin, what is the work of God's Spirit within us?

Another word for this transformation that God accomplishes in you is *sanctification*. Sanctification is the process by which you are molded into the image of Christ. It's the Spirit's progressive influence on you. Over time, day in and day out. He conforms and transforms your soul (your mind, will, and emotions: your heart) until it's increasingly operating in alignment with God's heart. And as the Spirit does His work, your thoughts and desires begin to inform and modify your actions and reactions. Your practice begins to align to the perfect nature of Christ in you.

Read James 1:21-22 in the margin and answer the following questions: How does the instruction from these verses accentuate practical righteousness? Be specific.

Recalling what you've learned this week about the spirit, soul, and body, what do you think James meant by "save your souls" (v. 21)?

Therefore, putting aside all filthiness and all that remains of wickedness, in humility receive the word implanted, which is able to save your souls. But prove yourselves doers of the word, and not merely hearers who delude themselves (Jas. 1:21-22).

Again, the process of sanctification is progressive. Just as a baby matures in stages—toddler to teenager to adult—God grows and changes us from one level to the next instead of all at once. In this way, our souls are consistently being "saved" as a part of our growth in God. Just as we were saved when we trusted in Christ and we will be saved at the day of judgment, it's equally true that we are being saved, more each day, from the person we used to be.

This process is so important and critical that when Paul wrote to the Christians at Philippi, he put it this way: "work out your salvation with fear and trembling" (Phil. 2:12). The people to whom he addressed the letter were already believers. They were already born again. Yet he said they still needed to exert some effort, in cooperation with the Holy Spirit's sanctifying work in them, as part of their salvation experience. And they'd better take it seriously.

SEEDS OF CHANGE

Why do you think James said we need to receive the Word that has already been implanted in us?

God is the One who softens and prepares the soil of our hearts, allowing the implanted Word to take effect (see Ezek. 36:24-32). But we still must make the choice to receive it. We must allow the Word to influence everything in our lives. When we do, it will work in sync with God's Spirit to organically cultivate internal health—a health that will inform, shape, and dictate our actions. Being merely a hearer of God's Word is not good enough. Millions of church attendees hear messages preached every Sunday and yet still live angry, unforgiving, deceptive lives. Why? Because hearing (while critical) doesn't achieve the same results as "receiving."

Meditating on the Word, internalizing its principles, and then implementing them in your actions is what supports the work of God's Spirit in renewing your soul. If you only skim Scripture while you're half asleep or as an afterthought, letting it go in one ear and out the other with little thought or interest, you'll never receive the full benefits of what the living, active Word of God is prepared to produce in your life. As we'll learn a bit later in this Bible study, God's Word is the Spirit's "sword." It's not only what He uses to grow you up and save your soul, but also to combat the enemy's attempts to do damage to you.

Choose one Scripture verse from your study this week that's particularly piqued your interest. How can you "receive" it instead of just reading it?

SAYING YES

As you begin to cooperate with the Holy Spirit in your sanctification by receiving the Word, you'll sense internal nudges prompting you to do things that align with light and conviction—and to not do things that align with darkness. You'll sense peace and divine approval when you're acting in a way that's pleasing to God—and uneasiness when you're not. This inner apprehension is called *conviction*. It's God's way of helping you put on your breastplate.

When was the last time you sensed conviction about something very specific in your life? What was your response?

Think through the next 24 hours. Can you anticipate an opportunity that will likely be coming up in which you can prepare now to say yes to the Spirit? Perhaps it's an interaction with a difficult person, and you can prepare now to be patient and pursue peace. Perhaps it's an area of indulgence where you can be proactive about exhibiting the self-control the Spirit will encourage you to display.

Remember, He never convicts for that which He doesn't also fully intend to empower. So receive the Word, heed His conviction, and watch your taste buds change in surprising ways as you grow in Him every single day.

Are there any behaviors or attitudes in your life that, honestly, you're doubtful you'll ever be able to change? Maybe you've tried for so long, you feel a complete sense of discouragement about it. Would you be bold enough to list them here?

No matter what you've written above, the Spirit can and will change you. Things you used to want, you'll lose an appetite for. Other things you never thought you'd want, you will begin to crave. Environments and conversations you could once tolerate and even enjoy despite undercurrents of evil will begin to feel uncomfortable and distasteful to you. And you, child of God, will start wearing that breastplate well.

Actionable Intel...

DAY 5
STRATEGY SESSION

For quite some time, the ancient Roman army did not establish a standardized, government-issued uniform for its soldiers. Those who could afford better gear could wear what they bought, but those who were poor went without and just hoped for the best. So in many cases, soldiers had no breastplate or coat of mail to protect their hearts.

Thankfully, the Lord has made sure nothing can keep us from going into battle under-dressed. The price of your breastplate was covered at Calvary. We'll never need to go out and purchase our own protection against the enemy. Hallelujah! Righteousness has been freely given to us in Jesus, so put it on!

As we come to the close of this beautiful week of study in the unchanging Word of our Almighty God, make a battle plan for wearing your breastplate. "Be imitators of God ... and walk in love, just as Christ also loved you and gave Himself up for us ..." (Eph. 5:1-2). The old man is dead and gone. You are no longer a slave to the flesh, to sin, to unrighteousness. You have been set free in Jesus and given new life.

Open your journal and build a strategy of thanksgiving to God for all He's done to make your breastplate available. Then ask Him for the ongoing, renewing strength of His sanctifying Spirit, as well as holy courage to wear this breastplate every day. Be honest about what you need to "put off" and "put on," then do it practically and consistently.

Remember, personalize your prayer. You can always refer to the Prayer Strategies on page 192 if you need to. Make your prayer unique to your specific circumstances and concerns. Include the promises of God and the instruction He's given you through your study this week to build a strategy that will put the enemy in his place and on the defeated fringes of your life every single time he hears you reading it out loud.

THE SHOES OF PEACE*

Consider the phrase "storms of life." What are some storms you've seen people you know face? How did the people respond?

Did anything about their responses surprise you? Disappoint you? Encourage you? Why?

Read John 16:33 aloud as you think about how you respond when you face tough times in your life. How might Jesus' words affect your response?

The storms of life will come. Sin and evil permeate our culture, our times, and our generation. Our enemy is very real. He may be invisible, but he is not fictional.

Now, read James 1:2. How does this verse challenge our usual attitude toward life's storms? Explain.

Throughout our study of Paul's Letter to the Ephesians, he's been teaching us to protect ourselves so we are able to stand firm against the enemy's schemes. Last week, we talked about the uniform Paul laid out for believers in Ephesians 6:13-15.

There are three items included in that uniform. List them below.
1.

2.

3.

We cannot survive the storms of life without the third part of our uniform: peace. But Satan wants us to be haunted by regret and guilt, overcome by our own weaknesses and failures. He wants our relationships characterized by division and discord. The enemy wants us peaceless so that when the storms of life come—even the ones that simply come because we live in a broken, sinful world—we'll be sucked under. Satan knows that where there is no peace, there is also no victory.

Let's remind ourselves about the truth of Satan's character. Read John 10:10 aloud. What do these verses teach us about our enemy? List his characteristics below.

That's why the apostle Paul knew we needed a reminder about the power God has given us. In Ephesians 6:10-15, he's told us to gird ourselves with truth and to put on the breastplate of righteousness. And then, he says, "Shod your feet with the preparation of the gospel of peace."

Roman soldiers wore a very distinctive shoe. It was a heavy military sandal that was sort of half boot and half sandal. They were made from leather and had open sections around the foot and ankle, and even upward around the leg, providing ventilation. But the most distinctive thing about these military sandals was that at the base of their tough leather soles, there were hobnails, steel posts that protruded from the bottom of the shoes. When the soldiers had to be able to stay upright, when the ground they were traversing was slick or steep, these nails would dig deeply down into the ground and enable the soldiers to stay upright and firm, no matter how difficult the terrain was they were seeking to traverse.

Life gets hard to travel. The road you're walking sometimes, it is going to be rocky. It's going to be slick. It's going to be easy for you to be knocked over and find yourself in a pool of despair. But when we have peace, the peace that can only be found in God, when it is anchored in our lives, it digs deeply into the soil of our existence and allows us to stay upright no matter how hard the winds may blow.

These shoes of peace that God is offering you will give you a firm grip. They will lock you in place so that you will not be knocked over. They will keep you sane when your world seems insane. They will allow you to stay upright and focused, able to still have healthy relationships even though you've been hurt in the past because you're not harboring all the resentment from past issues that you've dealt with. God's peace will keep you with sure footing no matter what is happening in your life.

Consider God's peace and what it does in our lives. Work together to fill in the following blanks.

- God's peace gives us a firm _____ which we need in a world that is not _____.

- God's peace gives us _____.

- God's peace allows us to keep our _____ when everything around us is swirling.

- God's peace will help to keep us _____.

Read Philippians 4:6-7 aloud. As a group, identify what this passage teaches us about God's peace.

How is the peace described in Philippians different from the world's concept of peace? Explain.

What things other than God do people trust to provide peace in their lives?

When God's peace is in your life, it will become your guard and your protector. Despite what the world thinks, true peace isn't found in success or fame or money. True peace—God's peace—is an inner tranquility and calmness of the soul. It's not something you can generate or achieve through all the things you do or have. God's peace anchors us, guards us, keeps us no matter what is happening around us. And the reality is if you have placed faith in Jesus Christ, you get peace, my friends. It is a gift of your salvation and of mine.

Read Ephesians 2:13-14. What do these verses reveal about God's peace? Explain in your own words.

The good news of the gospel is that Jesus has broken down the wall of sin that separated us from God. Our unholiness and God's holiness. Our imperfection and God's perfection. Jesus has bridged all of that.

In Jesus Christ, we have peace with God. Once and for all, when you accept Jesus Christ as savior, peace is established in your life. In Christ Jesus, those of us who were formerly far off are now brought near through the blood of Jesus.

That's good news.

Read John 14:27. Is God's peace something we create on our own? Explain.

God's peace is a gift of our salvation. If you are in Christ, His peace is already in you. But you have to activate it. Read Philippians 4:6 again to learn how. Write the answer below.

God instructed us to come to him with our requests—to be real with Him—but to pepper those requests with thankfulness. Our thankfulness activates the peace of God in our lives, which then acts as our guard and protector. But the only reason you can be thankful, even when you still have requests, is if you actually trust that no matter what's going on, God is still who He says He is, can do what He says He can do. So trust fuels thanksgiving, and thanksgiving activates peace.

What storms are you or someone you know facing today? How can you let your anxiety over those situations fuel thankfulness? Be specific.

Read Colossians 3:15. What else is peace supposed to do in our lives? Underline the answer in your Bible.

Peace is not only your guard and protector; it's also your guide. The word rule in this verse is of a presiding officer, like an umpire who decides whether a player has struck out. Peace tells you what is in bounds and what is out of bounds, when you're in the will of God and when you're out of His will. It is your umpire, helping you to discern the voice and the leading of God in your life.

Finally, standing firm doesn't necessarily mean you're in a stationary position. It might mean you are taking back what the enemy has taken from you, knocking down the strongholds he has created in your life. That's why you've got shoes, so that you can move forward. The peace of God tells you how to move.

So, trust. Be thankful. And walk forward in the shoes of peace this week with God as your guide!

DAY 1
MY FATHER'S SHOES

My youngest son loves to put on his father's gargantuan shoes and pretend to be grown up. They nearly swallow his little legs whole, but he clomps around the house like a Clydesdale, trying not to lose his balance and come tumbling down.

In years past, of course, if I'd come across size-thirteen, muddy footprints on the floor or if I tripped over a pair of my husband's shoes that had been left in the middle of the living room floor, I would've known exactly who the culprit was. I'd tell Jerry (nicely?) to please stop tracking dirt through the house or, better yet, kindly remove his shoes before coming in.

But, lately, there's just as good a chance a six-year-old is behind these prints—because when you're wearing your daddy's shoes, your footprints can start looking a whole lot like his.

This week, you and I are going to put on our Father's shoes. And by the Spirit's power, we are going to start seeing the tracks of peace He can make, not only in our own hearts, but also in our relationships and experiences with others. Perhaps the current status of things in your life makes you think no mere change of shoes can do anything to counteract the chaos and angst you're feeling and facing. But, yes—when those shoes are God's shoes, His footprints will start showing up everywhere you step.

Look at the typical shoes of the Roman soldier on the inside back cover. Write down the distinctive features you notice.

Why do you think these features might be important for a legionary going into battle?

After highlighting the belt and breastplate in Ephesians 6, Paul drew attention to the soldier's footwear, which was distinctive from other types of shoes from that time period. "Civilians wore soft leather shoes called *calcei*. Indoors, both sexes wore slippers, called *soleae*. Roman soldiers, however, wore heavy military sandals called *caliga*, half boot and half sandal."[1] The uppers were pierced with openwork designs, which "gave good ventilation, the many straps allowed adjustment to fit the peculiarities of an individual's foot, whilst parts of the boot that might rub (toe joints, ankle, big toe nail) were cut away."[2] The soles were made of several layers of leather and "were clenched with hobnails, frequently arranged in patterns."[3] These hollow metal studs provided a firm grip on the soil. We'll look at this in more depth tomorrow, but for now remember that these protrusions dug into the ground and kept the soldier sure-footed and stable when holding his ground or advancing against an enemy.

Turn to Ephesians 6:15 and write it word-for-word in the space below.

What spiritual virtue does Paul liken to this piece of the soldier's equipment? Record your answer beside the corresponding piece of armor on the inside back cover.

Picture yourself as a teacher of a Sunday school class filled with third grade children. One of them raises her hand and asks you to define *peace*. Write down the answer you give.

What words might you use to describe the opposite of peace? Why?

PRINTS OF PEACE

Of all the things the enemy seeks to steal, kill, and destroy in your life, peace is almost always near the top of his list. He intentionally stirs up discord, division, disruption, and disturbance, both within you and around you. He is the lord of chaos and confusion, using every opportunity to upset your sense of well being and stability. He wants you uneasy, unbalanced, filled with anxiety, worry, and turmoil. Lacking peace.

But there's more to it than that—because perhaps like no other attack, he knows that by nibbling away at your peace, he and his demonic entourage can cause his brand of tension to fan out in all directions, spreading out to your relationships, corroding them with disagreement and frustration.

Mark it down: whenever you feel an overriding sense of unrest inside or overwhelming distress in your relationships, the enemy is somewhere in the middle, stirring it up. Anywhere peace is lacking, you can be sure he's at work.

Read Digging Deeper 4 on page 122 to see how the armor permeates the entire Book of Ephesians.

Turn to page 122, which shows where each piece of the armor is explained throughout the Book of Ephesians. Record any distinction you notice about the primary references correlating to the "shoes of peace."

Remember, each of the pieces of armor are a mnemonic device of Paul's to summarize and remind the reader of what he'd already explained in his letter. Notice that every other piece of armor comprises between ten to thirty-five primary verses of earlier explanation. But in dealing with the topic of peaceable relationships, Paul's teaching covered forty-nine verses! It's not hard to see why: The strong, tangible presence of peace in our personal lives and our relationships is perhaps our most vital spiritual tool in threatening the success of the enemy's plans.

So naturally a big part of Satan's business involves stirring up turmoil in our hearts and relationships. Our own sins, of course, including past sins—though forgiven—provide him lots of working material for this task. As do the sins of others. If you've been the victim of abuse or injustice, for example, the enemy will ride the coattails of those wrongdoings to keep the pot boiling. He can turn simmering, low-lying anger into opportunities for unforgiveness, which then compound into bitterness and resentment. Then with these strongholds securely in place, you're much more likely to build emotional walls that even keep people with good intentions from being allowed into your heart. You become on edge, defensive, unable to foster authentic relationships.

One way or another, he's always out to steal your peace.

ANYWHERE PEACE IS LACKING, THE ENEMY IS AT WORK.
#ArmorOfGodStudy

In the following areas, list any ways you detect disharmony, unrest, or an overarching lack of peace. (We'll refer back to this exercise during our lesson today, so take your time. This is important.)

- your mind

- your heart

- your body

- between you and a friend

- between you and your parents

- between you and your siblings

- between you and your coworkers or teammates

- other

How have you seen the enemy's handiwork in these experiences? Explain.

How have you handled (or how are you generally handling) these situations?

CRIPPLED BY CHAOS

The most obvious benefit of the *caliga* was that it offered general protection for the feet. Without ample coverage, Roman soldiers would be susceptible to harm and injury while crossing rocky terrain—almost any terrain. And, hey, you can only go as far as your feet will take you. The result of having unguarded feet would leave them, if not out of commission, at least unable to stand firm for long periods or to move with agility and not become further impaired.

A life without peace is simply unprotected, crippled, unable to move forward, hindered from maturing and developing in a healthy fashion.

How have you witnessed a lack of peace crippling someone, rendering him or her incapable of moving forward in life?

In the areas of your life that you noted earlier, how have you seen your own potential or growth stunted because of this unrest in your heart or in your relationships? In what ways, if any, have you been unable to move forward?

No, we can't always control the kind of ground we're forced to march across. We may get a bad grade or cut from the team. We may get bad news from the doctor. We may get an upsetting message from a friend. We may have suffered abuse at the hands of another. None of these, just like none of the emotional and relational things you've been personally experiencing, is easy to deal with. And the enemy will always try to take advantage of experiences like these to gain access to your life. But with the right shoes on, you and I can be protected.

Shalom, the familiar Hebrew word for *peace* which permeates the Old Testament, does not refer to the absence of chaos, but rather to an overall, deeply entrenched sense of harmony, health, and wholeness in the midst of chaos. In fact, true peace is best detected and measured against the backdrop of commotion and confusion—when instability abounds, yet you remain steadfast; when disappointment and confusion are near, yet you're still capable of walking with Spirit-infused confidence, stability, and steadiness.

The Greek word for peace *in Ephesians 6:15 is* eirene, *the New Testament parallel to* shalom.

That's how you know your feet are fitted "with the preparation of the gospel of peace"—a peace beyond comprehension.

Go back and consider those areas of your life you commented on earlier. How did the enemy take advantage of an upsetting, unexpected, chaotic event or circumstance to gain access to your life?

Our enemy knows how easily we become incapacitated without our shoes of peace—unfit for warfare, unable to advance against him. He knows internal instability can keep us from being clearheaded and freehanded to fight against him—consumed with trying to grip onto the wrong things (anything!) to maintain our balance.

He knows turbulence and distance in our relationships will expose us to accusations of hypocrisy and lead us into misguided battles—causes we were never meant to fight for, hills we were never meant to die on.

But we can—we must—remain protected against this tactic, prepared to rise to our feet and move forward against the devil when divinely required to do so. This week, Paul provides some instructions to help us live abundantly, keep our sanity, and enjoy stability and balance in our lives no matter how upsetting our circumstances have been or will become.

If you were back in front of that Sunday school class, would you make any changes or additions to your earlier definition of *peace*? Record your expanded definition here.

Look back again to your personal list. Choose one of those items to consider in light of the following questions. If peace ruled your life:
1. **How would your behavior change in this situation?**
2. **In what way would your verbal responses change?**
3. **How would your ability to function physically be improved?**

As I write this last paragraph of today's lesson, I'm thinking about how you may have answered the previous questions. My heart is tender toward the one who hasn't slept well or eaten normally in weeks or months because you're in tremendous emotional or mental turmoil. I'm sensitive to the one whose most important relationships are in so much dysfunction that your ability to live well is affected sharply, the momentum of your life stunted. I am praying for you even now.

Yet I also feel a tinge of excitement as we launch into this week of our study because this week can revamp your entire life. The shoes that you and I are being offered and commanded to wear are God-sized, and they can leave footprints of peace in and through your life that you never thought possible. God's peace can keep your emotional footing sure, your mind and body stabilized, and your relationships intact.

Remember, a backdrop of commotion is the best place for the peace of God to be put on display. So if the enemy has been wreaking havoc all around you, and the chaos he's instigated has seemed to swallow you whole, don't be discouraged. Our God can and will anchor your soul, tethering it to the security found in His gospel, the good news of His beloved Son.

Hang on.

Peace is on the way.

Actionable Intel...

DAY 2
DIGGING IN

My boys love sports. No matter which one is in season, they want to play it. Basketball, football, baseball—they seem to have a hand in it all.

Or, should I say, a foot.

I'll admit it. I'm annoyed by the specialized footwear needed for each sport. The athletic shoes my sons "need" for basketball are somehow not suited for tennis. And the ones for soccer won't quite work for baseball. The truth is, they all look pretty much the same to me anyway.

But I know of one shoe with enough distinction from all the others that it makes me feel like I'm getting my money's worth. I believe the ancient Romans found it rather unique as well.

From Day 1, make a list of any characteristics of the *caliga* that were most memorable to you.

HOLES IN THE LINE

One of the most unforgettable features of a soldier's sandaled boots were the spikes that protruded from the thick leather soles, similar to the football cleats I bought for my boys last summer. These hobnails dug deeply into the earth, helping the soldier to hold his ground. To stand firm. Instead of slipping and sliding on slick terrain, causing their feet to be swept out from under them during intense struggle, the *caliga* offered firm footing.

This feature was also a critical factor in maintaining their battle line formations. The soldiers would stand shoulder to shoulder, one beside the other in a tight linear configuration, bringing strength to the whole. Impenetrable. Secure. The *caliga* kept each person in that line steady and strong, which meant the entire line was then steady and strong. If even one soldier lost his footing, the hole in the formation would weaken the line itself, leaving the whole army vulnerable to enemy attack.

From these four options, choose one Old Testament and one New Testament verse to study. In what sense can you, as an individual, expect God's peace to keep you steady and stable? Explain.

- Psalm 119:165
- Isaiah 54:10
- Luke 1:78-79
- Philippians 4:6-7

OK, good. Now I want you to broaden your perspective. Look back at the highlighted portion of the previous paragraph, and consider it within the context of the whole body of Christ. Remember, Paul's letter was written to the church at Ephesus. Sure, his instruction was directed to individuals, too, but his focus was on their relationship with each other.

Soldiers, by definition, operate as a unit. Gladiators competed as individuals, but a soldier could never be victorious without his companions. So when Paul outlined the armor that believers are to wear, he didn't only have individuals in mind. He was thinking of the living, breathing entity of the church as a whole. To the extent that individuals are armed for battle, so too the church—one believer united with another—is prepared to stand as one warrior, girded in God's power against the prince of darkness in the culture.

The church as a whole is armed only to the level that the members have armed themselves.
Philip Nation

Ephesians 4:1-16 goes into great detail about the church and why its internal unity is of paramount importance. Turn to this passage in your Bible. Read it slowly and then meet me back here.

How does the church benefit when the individuals within it pursue peace? Provide examples.

Have you seen the enemy breach the "holes in the line" of your local church? If so, how?

How about in the global church community—between denominations and segments of the church?

Using Ephesians 4:16 as a reference point, what would be the ill effects of a body that isn't "fitted and knit together"?

Jews and Gentiles of the first century were extremely antagonistic toward one another. Their history was filled with contention and offense. So they never could have imagined any scenario in which the two groups could unite in love and harmony. They had neither the desire nor the willingness. And yet the peace that Christ established on the cross was powerful enough to bridge even this colossal divide.

In Paul's letter to the Ephesians, he pointed to this relationship as proof of the extraordinary power of God's peace—not just in theory, but in personal practice. It was strong enough to establish stability and harmony then, and it is powerful enough to do it now.

Are hurt and anger lingering between you and another person? Between your church and another group across town? Between one race and another? The peace of God can bridge the gap and bring healing and restoration. And when it does, not only will it cause the people around here on this planet to sit up and notice, but it will declare the manifold wisdom of God through the church "to the rulers and authorities in the heavens" (Eph. 3:10, CSB). In other words, unity among once-divided brothers and sisters puts Satan promptly in his place.

Take time to stop and pray right now for your church. Ask the Lord to bridge any "holes in the line" and revitalize your congregation with a fresh passion for pursuing peace with one another.

BUMPY TERRAIN

The very fact that the soldier needed to don such specifically engineered footwear implied that his job required traversing some harsh terrain. Good traction and adhesion were crucial for victory. Since standing firm and maintaining the line could mean the difference between life and death for each soldier as well as his peers, only these shoes would do. An imitation would not be sufficient.

From him the whole body, fitted and knit together by every supporting ligament, promotes the growth of the body for building up itself in love by the proper working of each individual part (Eph. 4:16, CSB).

For he is our peace, who made both groups one and tore down the dividing wall of hostility (Eph. 2:14, CSB).

The terrain of Christian living can be rough, too. Dealing with other people in a way that is healthy and promotes peace requires a supernatural endowment that can only come from God Himself. Only these shoes—the shoes of peace—will do.

Prayerfully read Colossians 3:12-15 in the margin.

Ask the Lord to reveal to you people in your life who most need to experience each of the following from you. Record their names in the spaces provided. (It might need to be the same person for all of them.)

Compassion	
Kindness	
Humility	
Gentleness	
Patience	
Acceptance	
Forgiveness	
Love	

Some translate Colossians 3:13 this way—"accepting one another"—the implication being that the journey toward unity can often be difficult. Patience is a must. The terrain that leads toward restoring and maintaining peace with God's people can be like walking uphill, depending on their personality, weakness, and intentions.

But choose to do your part anyway. Hold the line so there won't be any holes where the enemy can take advantage. This does not mean you'll be best friends with everyone. It only means you'll be careful to make sure that unnecessary strife and division don't permeate and weaken the purposes of God. Then the church will be intact, strong, and ready to advance.

Turn to Ephesians 4, focusing on verses 1-3 and also verse 15. Record any similarities you detect from Colossians 3:12-15.

Walking in peace and pursuing it with others is Paul's prayer for us. End today's lesson by reading and receiving his hope and desire for all God's people:

> I pray that you, being rooted and firmly established in love, may be able to comprehend with all the saints what is the length and width, height and depth of God's love, and to know Christ's love that surpasses knowledge, so that you may be filled with all the fullness of God (Eph. 3:17-19, CSB).

Actionable Intel...

DAY 3

THE HOLE IN MY HEART

Big things are at stake this week—like your peace of mind, your ability to emotionally connect with those you love, your freedom from guilt and shame. And that's just the tip of the iceberg. Your most vital interpersonal relationships also hang in the balance, needing somebody like you to take a bold step to change the calculus of some really complex problems.

These shoes of peace can do a lot of walking (if we'll wear them) and take us to places we never thought we'd see in our lifetimes.

Only God's peace can dig in deep enough to offer the kind of anchoring, grounding, and security we need, keeping us from being knocked over and undone by a potent enemy who's always on the loose, and who specifically targets us in those areas where we're the weakest or most tender. False alternatives and cheap substitutes have never been and will never be sufficient replacements.

What kinds of alternatives have you seen people drawn toward as a substitute for true biblical peace?

What about you? What activities, people, or escapes do you tend to seek out when you're upset and trying to find peace?

In what way have you found these options to be …

- **temporary?**

- **unsatisfying?**

- **deceiving?**

… having shod your feet with the preparation of the gospel of peace (Eph. 6:15).

The only one who can truly satisfy the human heart is the One who made it.
Lois Evans

Every human being on the planet longs to be nurtured and filled with something—with Someone. But sadly, many people waste years of their lives seeking this fulfillment in relationships, substances, or ambitions, only to still be left feeling meaningless in the end. We know why, don't we? The vacuum within our hearts can only be occupied by the one thing for which it was created: relationship and intimacy with God.

We call this the gospel. But what we don't always as readily see or remember is how the peace it provides is a key component of our spiritual armor. So have I got some "good news" for you! The gospel never stops being a miracle—in more ways than one.

TWO TYPES OF PEACE

Two stages of peace are important to understand as we consider what it means to wear the shoes of peace when standing firm against the enemy. And both of them rest securely in the good news of the gospel.

1. Peace with God

2. Peace of God

How would you describe the difference between these two statements?

Last week, as we studied the breastplate of righteousness, we explored the chasm that exists between God and humanity, between His holiness and our unholiness, a breach that makes restoration and relationship with God unattainable by human effort alone. The dark extent of our sin nature means enmity and hostility are all that can exist between us and Him—unless somebody (not us) does something (what He did). Peace with God is only possible because of His unfathomable love for us.

Read Romans 5:1 in the margin. Underline the words "peace with God." Now rewrite the entire verse in your own words below.

Therefore, since we have been declared righteous by faith, we have peace with God through our Lord Jesus Christ (Rom. 5:1, CSB).

How does this verse accentuate what you learned about imputed righteousness last week (p. 78)?

How does imputed righteousness make peace with God possible?

That's the gospel—the declaration of our righteousness before God through Jesus Christ. The Greek word for *gospel* is *euaggelion*, which simply means *good news*—the best news we could ever hope to receive! When we place faith in Jesus Christ—in His death and resurrection—we are finally able to experience the intimacy with God our hearts were made for. Never again must we settle for unsatisfying substitutes that aren't capable of filling the void in our souls. Only Jesus—only the gospel—gives us true, forever peace.

That's why Paul so directly connected the gospel with the *caliga*. The supernatural power for standing firm under the mounting pressures of daily life is only possible through the deep-seated sense of peace and confidence found in a saving relationship with God. Without it? No hope. Not a chance.

I've often wondered how anyone survives who doesn't have a settled conviction that this earth is not their home. Everything here is unstable and inevitably disappointing. Grades can plunge, boyfriends or girlfriends can disappoint, dreams can disappear, friends can fail, death can claim our loved ones. If our emotional state is directed by the shifting circumstances of earth, we will constantly be in a state of turmoil and confusion. We need an anchor in our soul that keeps us stable and sound or we're done.

Peace with God is the answer. The only answer. But praise God, an available answer. An ever-present answer. An everlasting answer.

Recall a time when you saw hopelessness collapse around someone who didn't have peace with God. What was one of the most noticeable things you remember about what he or she did? What you saw?

> **THE MAIN MESSAGE AND CONTENT OF THE GOOD NEWS IS PEACE.**
> *#ArmorOfGodStudy*

Slowly and carefully read Ephesians 2:13-14. How does Paul emphasize the way peace with God should affect our relationships with others?

The gospel doesn't only stabilize our own hearts, it makes stability possible even with the most unlovable and difficult people we encounter. I mean, come on, it's not like we're the most lovable all the time either, right? And yet, "while we were yet sinners" (Rom. 5:8), Christ loved us enough to bridge the gap between us and the Father. "He came and preached peace to you who were far away, and peace to those who were near" (Eph. 2:17). To you and to me and ... yes, to them too. So how dare we not extend the same grace, forgiving them just as He's forgiven us. He'll empower us to do it every single time. This is where the peace of God comes in.

THE PEACE OF GOD

Our salvation is not just about going to heaven and escaping hell. Those are certainly the most extraordinary benefits of our relationship with Jesus, but if our concept of salvation ends there, we're selling it short. Peace with God establishes our relationship with Him, and as a result, we can experience the peace of God. This is what makes peace a legitimate option for us right now, on earth.

Turn to Galatians 5:22-23 and write in the margin all the fruit of the Spirit listed there.

Think back to your study of Ephesians 4 and Colossians 3 from the end of Day 2. Circle any of the fruit of the Spirit that show up in both passages.

God's Spirit indwells you at the moment of salvation (Eph. 1:13). His job is not only to sanctify you (which we looked at last week), but also to empower you to develop and exhibit His fruit. So when God's Spirit came into your life, He brought housewarming presents—a nice fruit basket, plus an array of personalized gifts for you to use in serving

> SALVATION ISN'T JUST ABOUT HEAVEN. IT'S ABOUT BEING EMPOWERED ON EARTH.
> *#ArmorOfGodStudy*

others. As Jesus said to His disciples before His death, and ultimately before returning in resurrected glory to the Father: "Peace I leave with you; My peace I give to you; not as the world gives do I give to you. Do not let your heart be troubled, nor let it be fearful" (John 14:27).

So, you see, the anchoring and guiding peace of God is already in you as a divine gift. Your task is to make sure it's not lying dormant, unused, and unappreciated. You must choose to cultivate and activate it in your life.

But how? How do you put on the shoes of peace? Let's take a walk through three passages of Scripture that teach us how—two from the New Testament and one from the Old.

First, turn to Philippians 4:6-7 in your Bible. What causes the peace of God to guard your heart in a way that surpasses all comprehension?

NOTE THE PROGRESSION: TRUST LEADS TO THANKFULNESS AND GRATITUDE ACTIVATES PEACE.

#ArmorOfGodStudy

Now, turn to Colossians 3:15, which shows peace as our guide. What is the last directive given in this verse?

Finally, turn to Isaiah 26:3-4. As closely as you can do it from your translation, fill in the blanks below.

The steadfast of mind You will keep in _____ _____, because he trusts in You. _____ in the _____ forever, for in God the Lord, we have an _____ Rock.

When we choose thankful prayer over wallowing in anxiety and worry, we are demonstrating an unwavering trust in God. Prayer shrouded in gratitude expresses a firm faith. Concentrating on Him instead of being absorbed by our circumstances tells the Lord that we believe He is able to override and overcome even the most difficult issues. This kind of faith catches His attention, and He responds by activating His peace within us—a peace that will not only guard but also guide us by helping us to discern the direction God is leading us to take in our lives.

Record at least three specific things for which you can be grateful to God, despite whatever difficulty you're currently facing.

How can you incorporate these three things into your prayer strategy this week? Be specific.

When God sees this type of prayerful, grateful faith, when our mind is centered on Him, the peace of God expands within us. It stabilizes our emotions, centers our minds, guides our footsteps, and overflows into our experience with others.

This is how we put on the shoes of peace—we trust and express gratitude. Then, we experience the peace of God that surpasses all understanding.

Starting today, any time you feel worry or anxiety creeping into your heart, take it as your cue to turn your attention to God. Pray. Trust Him. Be grateful. And watch His peace—a peace you cannot even begin to explain—swell in your experience. Then your feet will be fitted with the *shalom* of God.

> *May the Lord of peace himself give you peace always in every way. The Lord be with all of you (2 Thess. 3:16, CSB).*

Actionable Intel...

DAY 4

GO SHOES

A few years ago, my husband and I had the joy of going on a vacation with several of our friends. During one of our meals, we starting talking about the differences between guys and girls when it comes to packing for trips. All the guys had brought only one suitcase, while all the girls brought least two. The consensus among the women was that shoes took up the most of the space.

One of the women admitted that she had forgotten to pack any tennis shoes. "I hope we don't have anything too active planned," she said. "I don't have the shoes for that!"

One of the guys, shaking his head, responded, "All those dress shoes ... and no go shoes." No. Go. Shoes.

Spiritual warfare calls for shoes that are appropriate for the occasion. But often our spiritual lives are so full of religious activity designed to impress others that we forget to pack the basic requirements, the ones that will actually support victory.

We need more go shoes—the kind that make us ready and prepared for battle. Having your feet fitted with the peace that the gospel brings, and that the Spirit uses to guide you onward, makes you ready for anything the enemy tries to send your way.

The Greek word translated preparation or readiness in Ephesians 6:15 is used nowhere else in the New Testament, but it does occur several times within the Septuagint (the Greek version of the Old Testament). Its implication is of being sure-footed and established. Ready to go.

From Day 3, review the difference between peace with God and the peace of God. How do they work together to make us "ready" and "prepared" to stand firm?

PEACE PUBLISHERS

Don't forget, now, that our armor is Yahweh's own armor. Most of what Paul described in Ephesians 6 is lifted directly from the vivid imagery of the Divine Warrior meticulously painted in the Book of Isaiah. While the "shoes of peace" are not specifically mentioned alongside the other pieces of armor in those key passages (Isa. 11:5; 59:17), many scholars suggest they are closely related to the purpose and message of Yahweh's Messiah as described by the Old Testament prophet.

Turn to Isaiah 52:7. What correlation do you detect between the picture of the Messiah in this verse and those from Ephesians in the margin?

He came and proclaimed the good news of peace to you who were far away and peace to those who were near (Eph. 2:17, CSB).

Isaiah wasn't painting the picture of someone standing still, passing the time, waiting for the right opportunity to get up and go. No, his go shoes are on. He is running toward Jerusalem, eager to share the good news. His feet are described as beautiful and lovely—and in motion. These feet carry a message of salvation and hope to all people. And "as he comes within earshot of the city he shouts 'peace,' 'good tidings,' 'salvation,'" the content of which is amplified by "Your God reigns."[5] The messenger is alert and ready, prepared to declare peace to everyone.

... your feet sandaled with readiness for the gospel of peace (Eph. 6:15, CSB).

This means standing firm against the enemy is not merely a defensive posture. Yes, victory has already been won for us by the cross and Calvary. Yes, we are to plant our spiritual feet on that hard-won ground and secure our post. But standing firm is not only about digging in; it's also about moving forward. It's about going into enemy territory from a strong position of victory and taking back ground he's sought to steal.

Read 2 Corinthians 10:4-5 in the margin. Underline all the benefits and outcomes our divinely ordained weapons are designed to achieve.

Throughout this study, if the Holy Spirit has brought to your attention an area of your life that is out of alignment with Him—where the enemy has erected strongholds, embedded lies, or enslaved you to sin through his personalized temptations—realize that this armor and these weapons we're learning about can do more than just dig in. They can actually dig a stronghold out and advance against the enemy in victory. They are active and potent.

The weapons of our warfare are not of the flesh, but are powerful through God for the demolition of strongholds. We demolish arguments and every proud thing that is raised up against the knowledge of God, and we take every thought captive to obey Christ (2 Cor. 10:4-5, CSB).

Our peace shoes are go shoes. They are designed to move forward and announce the good news of victory. Powerful enough to tear down, demolish, and take back. They can go into the territory of your life that may currently be under enemy influence and get it back in Jesus' name.

> *"How beautiful upon the mountains are the feet of him who brings good news, who publishes peace, who brings good news of happiness, who publishes salvation, who says to Zion, 'Your God reigns'" (Isa. 52:7, ESV).*

Yes, you are a publisher of peace, a messenger of the good news. Through God's Word, you can declare freedom and peace over your own circumstances and even the lives of those you love. You can shout "our God reigns" until He actually does reign in your mind and heart and circumstances. Your feet have been made ready by the gospel. Now go!

What are some areas of your life where you need to be on the offensive instead of the defensive, taking back ground from the enemy?

What would this process look like in a practical sense? Prepare to discuss this with your group.

ONWARD

Too often, we've complicated the spiritual privilege of sharing the gospel into rehearsed, programmatic deliveries, always headed toward the sinner's prayer. God bless all those who share the good news of Jesus, in whatever way God leads them to do it. But a lot of us just need to let God's peace do what God's peace does. Allow His Spirit to naturally guide us in living and sharing the blessings of gospel peace with those around us as we submit to His leadership and promptings.

When we begin to see the supernatural effects of the gospel, the result should be gratitude that overflows into action. We should be people who go into the enemy's territory and freely tell others of the victory that can be theirs in Jesus. A lot of them want it more than we know. More than even they realize.

Listen, the greatest threat to the growth of the kingdom of darkness in our culture is the expansion of the kingdom of light. When we carry this message to others and the community of faith grows, the enemy will be pushed back.

Ask the Lord to reveal to you a person with whom you can proactively share the message of the gospel in the coming days. Write his or her name below.

What steps can you take toward engaging this person?

Historians tell us, in thinking back to ancient Roman warfare: given the hobnails at the base of the soldiers' shoes, "an army marching along a stone-paved road must have created a considerable clatter."[6] The enemy would've known they were coming.

... having shod your feet with the preparation of the gospel of peace (Eph. 6:15).

Actually, this effect was by design. Their armor "served not only to protect but to impress and intimidate. It represented the character and strength of the warrior and symbolized his past and present actions."[7]

Peace intimidates our enemy. He knows we're coming when we're all marching in unity with our peace-shoes securely in place. The sound will let him know that we are ready, at our post, standing our ground, and fearlessly advancing against his kingdom. And, that's good news.

So, march on, my friend.

> *Therefore as you have received Christ Jesus the Lord, so walk in Him (Col. 2:6).*

Actionable Intel...

DAY 5

STRATEGY SESSION

My friend Lisa went skydiving for her fiftieth birthday. She'd always wanted to try it, so she did. I was so proud of her for taking the risk and doing something so adventurous. Later she told me all about it—the blood-rushing, energy-charged descent of the initial free fall, and then the serene, steady drop after the parachute had been opened.

She also told me how, more than anything, she was thankful for the instructor. She hadn't left him behind in the plane she'd jumped out of. No way! He was strapped to her back. No matter how fast she was falling through the air, no matter how rapidly the approaching ground seemed to be nearing, no matter how loud and intimidating the air in the atmosphere sounded as it whipped through her hair, she felt safe and assured and could even smile—right there in the middle of a free fall through the sky. Why? Because she was safely tethered to someone who knew exactly what he was doing.

This, in essence, is an accurate portrait of peace. It is your instructor, guiding you, keeping you steady, assured, unwavering, even capable of smiling when everything in your environment says you should be screaming for dear life.

That's the spiritual confidence that comes from peace.

Consider the peace continuum below. Where would you rank today? Mark an X on the place you think best describes your state of peace.

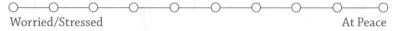

Worried/Stressed   At Peace

Explain your answer.

I don't know where you stand today on the peace continuum—whether you're smoothly sailing through your various struggles right now, or you're nearly biting your nails to the quick and biting people's heads off for every little perceived offense. Or somewhere in between. But as you begin asking the Lord for direction on drawing up a personal prayer strategy for sliding into the shoes of peace, I want you to consider a little field-trip exercise:

Think of a person you know whose life is peace-filled. Write his or her name below and describe how you've seen this virtue reflected in his or her life against the backdrop of difficult circumstances. Also, describe how you've seen it offer protection against the enemy's attempts to stunt that person's progress. How have you seen him or her thrive despite difficulty?

One of the most impactful things I've ever done is to call a person whose peaceful life I admire to ask how she has effectively applied the peace of God to her life. Consider reaching out to the person you've listed. Listen, learn, and record insights in your journal.

I think you just might find the beginnings of your prayer strategy when you do.

THE ARMOR IN THE BOOK OF EPHESIANS

The apostle Paul's delineation of the armor in Ephesians 6 is simply a reiteration—a summary of principles he has already discussed beforehand in his letter. Each piece has been introduced and thoroughly explained earlier. This is why his comments about them at the end of the letter are so concise and succinct. The sword of the Spirit is the only article he defines along with its mention, by identifying it as "the Word of God" (v. 17).

On the next page you will find a list of each piece of armor, along with the passages that are primarily and secondarily connected to it throughout the book.

It is interesting to note that while Ephesians 6 lists the armor in the order that a Roman soldier would have put each piece on, Paul's explanation of them throughout the letter is in reverse order—starting with the helmet and ending with the belt.

Food for thought: In the original language, the first four pieces of armor are introduced with words and phrases that modify the command to "stand" in verse 14. Paul's intention was to clarify the means by which one can stand against the powers of darkness. They do so by being girded in truth, righteousness, peace, and faith.

After reviewing the chart, turn back to our Ephesians passage on page 7. Draw an arrow from each of the first four pieces of armor to the imperative "stand" in verse 14. This will be your constant reminder of Paul's intent to teach you how to stand firm against the insidious schemes of the devil.

Armor	Ephesians 6 Reference	Additional References
Sword of the Spirit	Eph. 6:17	
Helmet of salvation	Eph. 6:17	**Eph. 1:1-23**; 2:5,8; 5:23
Shield of faith	Eph. 6:16	**Eph. 2:1-10**; 1:1,13,15,19; 3:12,17; 4:5,13
Shoes of peace	Eph. 6:15	**Eph. 2:11–4:16**; 1:13
Breastplate of righteousness	Eph. 6:14	**Eph. 4:17–5:9**
Belt of truth	Eph. 6:14	**Eph. 5:8–6:9**; 1:13; 4:15,21-25
Prayer	Eph. 6:18,19	**Eph. 1:16,18**; 3:14-18

WEEK 5

THE SHIELD OF FAITH

Think about the old adage "Actions speak louder than words." What do you think that saying means?

Based on your understanding of that phrase, when have you seen someone's actions speaking louder than words?

What do you think the idea—that actions speak louder than words—has to do with faith? Explain.

Now, read James 2:20,26 aloud. How has your answer changed?

Faith without works is useless. Faith without works is dead.

You can have all the faith in the world, but if there's no work on your part to connect with it, then you will never see the results.

In this passage of James, the original Greek word used for faith is the word *pistis*. I want you to know that because this exact same word is the word that Paul used in the passage that you and I have been looking at over the course of the last four weeks.

Read Ephesians 6:10-19 again as a group, paying attention to each piece of armor that's listed. Underline the word faith in verse 16.

In Ephesians 6:16, Paul tells us the next piece of armor that you and I need to wield in order to stand firm against the schemes of the devil: the shield of faith. Every single time this word is used in the New Testament—which, by the way, is more than 200 times—we see this original word, *pistis*. The word relates to the action of a person, to the activity involved in the belief system of an individual. So, when Paul told us to take up the shield of faith, he was calling us to actively exercise our faith. Active faith is a shield in our lives.

In light of what you read, consider the word *faith*. How would you define it? Write it in your own words below and discuss with the group.

Remember how we've talked about the first three pieces of the armor of God as a uniform, as attributes or characteristics that describe us? Take note of how the language changes in verse 16. For the belt of truth, the breastplate of righteousness, and the shoes of peace, we're told to "gird our loins," "put on," and "shod our feet." For these final three, Paul uses more active commands.

Reread Ephesians 6:16-19. Underline the verbs Paul used when teaching about the shield of faith, helmet of salvation, and sword of the Spirit. What do these active commands teach you about how you are supposed to utilize these pieces of armor?

We are called to an active faith. Our faith isn't just believing what God says is true; it's acting on it. Faith is what you say you believe *in action*. Faith is when you act like God is telling the truth.

Let's consider what active faith reveals about our relationship with God. Fill in the blanks below.

1. **Faith reveals a _____ on God.**

2. **Faith is what you say you believe in _____.**

3. **Faith is when you _____ like God is telling you the _____.**

The truth is, faith actually says less about us and more about what we believe to be true about God. Because if we really believe He is faithful like we say we do, if we really believe that He is trustworthy, then we will step out in faith. That's the indicator of what we really believe.

Think about sitting in a chair. You can talk about how you believe the chair will support you until you're blue in the face, but you don't put your faith in that chair until you actually sit in it. You don't experience the benefits of the chair until you actually rest your weight on it. The truth is, we will never see the benefits of our faith and our relationship with God unless we are willing to marry our faith with our actions.

Have you or someone you know ever walked through a tough time or a situation in life that caused you to question God's faithfulness? Why do you think it was tempting to doubt God's faithful character in that season? Explain.

Even if we may sometimes doubt it, God is faithful. Just consider the fact that when He was born, when He was just a tiny baby wrapped in swaddling clothes, Jesus Christ had already fulfilled countless Old Testament prophecies concerning the Messiah. So in His first breath as an infant, Jesus had already proven His faithfulness. And if He could do that as a baby, can you imagine how profound, vast, great, lavish, and abounding all His faithfulness really is?

Because He is faithful, you and I can have active faith. We can believe that what He has called us to, He will equip us for. We sell Him short when we don't trust Him enough to believe that.

Read Ephesians 6:16 again. What did Paul say the shield of faith would help believers to do?

In ancient warfare, armies would often send flaming arrows—more like javelins, really—into the ranks of the enemy. These flaming arrows weren't meant to kill or injure (although they could and did); they were meant to distract. If the enemy could get a fire burning in the camp, it would distract some of the soldiers and create a break in the ranks where the enemy could infiltrate.

What are some distractions you've seen Satan try to use to infiltrate your life or the lives of those you love? Discuss your thoughts as a group.

Read 2 Timothy 1:7 aloud. How have you seen the enemy use this tactic to distract believers from stepping out in faith to follow Him?

One of the enemy's primary schemes is to cripple us in fear. The opposite of faith isn't faithlessness; it's fear. It's what keeps us worrying about all the "what-ifs" rather than moving forward in faith, trusting that if God has called us to something, He is faithful to equip us to accomplish it.

Our enemy wants to keep us from stepping out in faith because he knows the minute we do—when we activate that shield of faith—we will be protected and his fiery arrows will be extinguished.

Think about what we've been learning the past few weeks. Is there something God has convicted you of or something He's been calling you to do through your study of His Word? How does what we've learned today challenge you to respond?

Listen, whatever He's called you to do, you do it. Has He asked you to participate in that organization or forgive that person? Has He asked you to start a Bible study group or join a ministry? To reach out to that guy or girl on your team, at work, or in your class? Whatever He has asked you to do, once you step out in faith, the shield goes up.

Let's consider something I like to call "The Faith Place." Read Luke 5:1-11 in your Bible. How did Simon exhibit faith in these verses? Considering the circumstances, why would it have been easy for him to doubt Jesus or even refuse to step out in faith?

Simon had fished all night and caught nothing. He'd already washed his nets and given up for the day. He knew, as all fishermen did, that you didn't really catch fish in the middle of the day on the Sea of Galilee, and if you did, it was in the shallow water. Yet here was Jesus telling him to go out into the deep water and cast out his net.

Consider verse 5. Simon had come to "The Faith Place." He was stepping out in faith, putting himself into a position where God would have to come through. When have you seen someone step out with that kind of faith? What did you learn from that experience?

Simon had to determine to do what God had called him to do, even though it went against his own understanding, his feelings, and what rationality told him to do. What Jesus asked him to do didn't make sense, but Simon did it anyway. And he had to take action to do so. He had to cast out the net, even though Jesus, God Himself, could have called for the fish to simply jump in the boat.

That's active faith.

That's what this week of your Bible study is about. It's about calling to your mind what the Holy Spirit has been convicting and challenging you to do, how He has been asking you to step out in faith. Put your faith to work this week. Let it be active. Activate the shield of faith in your life and let Him conquer the fear and extinguish the distractions.

DAY 1
REAL FAITH

I'd watched her for a while—carefully, steadily. This woman from my Bible study group was different, unusual somehow. Radiating with the power of God. Overwhelmed with His joy and consumed with His peace. Not just occasionally, but always. Her interaction with God was ongoing and relational. The Word was alive to her—because God was alive to her.

This woman was one of the few people I'd ever met who actively saw evidence of God's activity in the rhythms of her life. She would pray and then believe. Expect and then see. Ask and then receive. She was not easily discouraged or paralyzed by fear and insecurity, and she had a laundry list of very practical experiences with God to prove it.

That's why I couldn't wait for the chance to sit down and share a lunch with her. Not to talk, but to listen. I left that meal with a full stomach and heart, wanting more than anything to have a life that mirrored hers. The secret she shared with me that day is the exact same one I want to reveal to you during this fifth week of Bible study. All of it can be summed up in one tiny but very critical, power-filled word: FAITH.

How would you describe the difference between belief and faith?

Generally speaking, what do you think are the biggest obstacles to believers acting in faith?

FULL COVERAGE

The first-century Roman army was the most advanced in the ancient world. And their success can be attributed to the fact that no other army possessed such intricately designed armor. Their sandaled shoes studded with hobnails on the bottom, their sturdy breastplate, and their solid, supportive girdles gave them a clear advantage in battle. Additionally, the Roman soldiers received extensive training in their unique linear formation which, when exacted with precision, made them virtually impenetrable and impassable. Yet the piece of equipment they were most known for was their shield.

Turn to the image on the inside back cover and familiarize yourself with the soldier's shield. Write down the corresponding spiritual virtue in the blank beside it, then meet me back here.

There were two types of shields used by soldiers during this time frame. The one the apostle Paul was describing in Ephesians 6 was not a small, round one—about the size of a trash can lid—that left most of the soldier's body uncovered and exposed. He was referencing a larger shield that was typically two feet wide and four feet long, shaped almost like a door, consisting of planks of wood fused together. The wood was covered by canvas. Then by leather. Then iron was built into the center as a hub and also onto the extreme edges of the shield from top to bottom. This made the shield able to withstand the hard-hitting strokes of an enemy's broadsword during close combat. Ancient historians say these shields were so large they were capable of covering the whole body of a soldier when he was crouched down.

Choose one of the following examples that show someone exhibiting faith and receiving divine protection as a result. Answer the following questions for the example that you choose to study.

- **The children of Israel (Ex. 11:4-7; 12:5-7,13)**
- **Daniel (Dan. 6:7-10,16-23)**
- **Rahab (Josh. 2:8-21; 6:24-25)**

How did the people in these passages demonstrate confidence in God?

How were they protected as a result of their obedience?

Is there any instance from your own experience when you felt specifically protected by God as a result of having acted in faith?

He is a shield to those who take refuge in Him (Prov. 30:5).

The unique, oblong shield of the Roman soldier was called a scutum.[1]

Faith is one of the most overused and yet underused expressions in Christian circles. Which is completely backward. Because really, talking about faith is not the same as having it. In the example you studied, the true meaning of faith is clearly revealed. Plain and simple, faith is an action. That's the secret my friend shared with me over lunch that day.

Look at the verses from James in the margin. How does James's illustration using the human body and spirit help explain the concept of faith and works more clearly?

Faith without works is useless ... For just as the body without the spirit is dead, so also faith without works is dead (Jas. 2:20,26).

When I pressed my friend for details on her walk with the Lord, she talked about how often she "takes up" the shield of faith by doing what God has asked her to do, no matter how risky or intimidating the circumstances. From giving a gift to a stranger or being the first to mend fences with a friend to larger, more life-altering things—like moving from one state to another—her commitment to quickly engage this piece of weaponry, she said, was the key that not only unlocked the door to spiritual vibrancy, but also kept her from falling prey to the enemy's attacks. As far as she could tell, what separated her experience with God from so many others was that she was willing and committed to translate her beliefs to active faith—acting on the promises and directives of God, not just talking about them. It certainly wasn't easy, but over time she'd learned to trust God enough to move forward at His word.

Pistis (pronounced pē'-stēs) is the transliteration for the word faith used by James. It is the same word used by the apostle Paul in Ephesians and again over 200 times in the New Testament. In almost every instance, it relates to a person's action.

Turn to Hebrews 11:1 and copy this biblical definition of faith word-for-word below.

The word *evidence* or *conviction* in Hebrews 11:1 is translated from the Greek word *elanchos* (pronounced "e'-len-khos"), meaning *proof*. Faith is "proof of that which is not seen." Consider what it means to have "proof" of something. How does this understanding help us see faith as a tangible thing rather than an invisible virtue?

If the definition of faith in Hebrews 11:1 is different from the personal definition you wrote at the beginning of today's study, adapt your new definition here.

Any faith that must be supported by the evidence of the senses is not real faith.[2]
A. W. Tozer

BY DEFINITION

Simply put, faith is acting like God is telling the truth. The key thought here is action. By definition, faith is not talking about or thinking about or even celebrating God's truth. It is the process of adapting your behavior, your decisions, and ultimately, your whole lifestyle so that it accords with what God has asked you to do—without needing to see the evidence that it will all work out in the end. In fact, the thing that makes faith, well, faith, is when—like Daniel, Rahab, and the children of Israel—you choose to act in accordance with truth despite the fact that you can't see what the outcome will be. The act of faith is what becomes a shield of protection to guard against the enemy's attacks.

Underline the key words and phrases in the paragraph above.

As my dad and pastor, Dr. Tony Evans, says, faith is acting like it is so, even when it is not so, so that it might be so, simply because God said so.

End today by making a list of any areas where you sense God asking you to take a step of faith right now—either because it's a clear directive from His Word (to forgive, to tithe, etc.), or because you feel the leading of God's Spirit. We'll refer back to this list again throughout the week.

FAITH IS ACTING LIKE GOD IS TELLING THE TRUTH.
#ArmorOfGodStudy

If you've hesitated to move forward in obedience—why? Try to narrow down and document your reasons here.

If this matter is something directly addressed in God's Word, list some of the Bible references below.

If the directive you've listed is not directly addressed in the Bible, have you ...

- prayed fervently about it?
- made certain it aligns with the overarching themes and direction revealed in Scripture and will in no way manipulate or go against it?
- asked for wise counsel from someone in spiritual authority in your life?

Now, apply the four elements of my dad's definition of faith to this area of your life. Record your thoughts for each one.

Faith is:

- Acting like it is so (In what practical way can you respond in faith?);
- Even when it is not so (What are the unseen elements that make it difficult to do so?);
- So that it might be so (What are God's promises to you?);
- Simply because God said so (What has He told you to do?).

While faith often requires risk, it also incorporates wisdom. Wise believers seek sound direction, clarity, and confirmation before moving forward so they aren't making impulsive or foolish decisions. In fact, the more your choice will alter your lifestyle or affect others around you, the more time, effort, and energy you should spend confirming God's Word before you do anything. But once you get clarity on what you believe God requires of you, your very next step is faith. That's your shield—covering and protecting you from the evil one.

Actionable Intel...

DAY 2
ON FIRE

Throughout the history of warfare, one of the tactical practices designed for maximum disruption was the staging of a surprise assault using flaming arrows. These arrows, lit aflame at their ends, would flail through the air toward their intended targets (for example, the canvas wagons and tents of a military campsite), setting everything ablaze.

And, man, was it effective. If enough of those arrows hit enough of those targets, the whole brigade of soldiers would be busy trying to quell the blaze before it burned through all their gear and supplies.[3] Distracted by the flames, the men became vulnerable by becoming preoccupied, too distracted to deal with whatever follow-up attack their oncoming enemy was planning next.

In Day 1, you ended your lesson by pinpointing areas of your life in which you sense God asking you to step out in faith with confidence in His ability to see you through. If you've felt distracted from and hesitant about moving forward, circle any of the following reasons that apply to you.

insecurity · fear · doubt · temptation · anxiety/worry about "what ifs" · sudden increase of other stressful life circumstances · discouragement/questioning your ability · guilt · hopelessness · hateful thoughts about another person · other

Your enemy wants to distract you, so he can blindside you. His strategy is tailored. Do you think whatever you circled in the exercise above is happenstance, somehow unrelated to the specific attacks of the enemy against you? No, he's studied your tendencies and habits, your deepest fears and weaknesses, and has aimed at those areas in particular. He knows he can't destroy you. You're eternally secure in Jesus. But he fully intends to sidetrack your attention by setting any number of internal fires ablaze in your life—like insecurity, intimidation, of internal fires ablaze in your life—like insecurity, intimidation, anxiety, worry, or busyness. He wants you to contemplate disobedience, entertain crippling doubts, and burden your conscience with paralyzing accusations so you'll be unfocused while he sneaks up from behind.

Thinking of the particular struggle you circled, how has it caused you to be distracted and sidetracked from doing God's will?

How else have you noticed the enemy creeping in and blindsiding you—perhaps in other areas of your life—while you've been preoccupied with putting out these internal fires?

Think back to the difficult person or circumstances you wrote down in the oval during week one of our study. What, if any, connection do you see between the step of faith God is asking you to take and that situation? Explain.

Roman armies faced "flaming missiles" from their opponents as well—except they were called *plumbatae*, and were more like the javelins you see in modern Olympic games, with the tips coated in pitch and set on fire. They were often referred to as "darts," but big ones, sometimes launched by a catapult to give them sufficient velocity and accuracy. But the objective was the same: distraction, diversion, chaos. If enough of these darts lodged successfully in their target, their opponents would no longer be able to advance against them.

But the Romans had an answer for this kind of attack. And so do you.

FIRE EXTINGUISHER

The "shield of faith" was especially important to the apostle Paul. Know how I know? Because, other than prayer, he put more of an emphasis on this piece of armor than any of the others, by including additional statements before and after mentioning the shield itself.

Read the passage in the margin and underline the statements surrounding the "shield of faith" that reveal Paul's emphasis.

Why do you think Paul may have gone to greater lengths to accentuate the benefits of this piece of equipment? Prepare to discuss this with your group.

In addition to all, taking up the shield of faith with which you will be able to extinguish all the flaming arrows of the evil one (Eph. 6:16).

First, Paul described the benefits of using it. With the other pieces of armor, we're left to discover the benefits for ourselves by studying other portions of the letter. But with the shield, in addition to referring to it earlier—when talking about faith in Ephesians 2:1-10—Paul tells us right away what the results will be when we employ the shield.

Also, the phrase "in addition to all" provides a linguistic break in the passage that prepares us for something new and distinct from his explanation of the first three pieces.

Turn to Ephesians 6 and compare verses 14-15 with 16-17. What major difference do you detect in the tone of these two sections? Write your observations below.

With the belt, breastplate, and shoes, he conveys them as a spiritual uniform that should be worn by believers at all times. Minute by minute. Day by day. But he approaches this piece of equipment differently. With the shield, he commands for it to be "taken up."

Look at it this way: A nurse might wear scrubs every day to work because it's his or her uniform. But when the need arises, he or she will pick up a stethoscope, thermometer, or any number of tools to use on a patient. Likewise, we must always wear our daily, divinely given uniform, but also be prepared to "take up" the other tools when required.

The first of these pieces of armor is the shield of faith. The moment when we first sense a flaming *plumbata* infiltrating our life in some way, we activate faith as a shield of protection over our lives.

So don't miss the irony here. The enemy sends flaming arrows into your life specifically when you are being called to walk in faith. Those arrows are deliberately intended to disable you from doing the only thing that has the power to extinguish them: walking in faith! The enemy knows that if you'll ever push past the insecurity, doubt, or fear that's burning in your soul, choosing instead to believe God's truth and walk in accordance with it, you'll erect a shield of protection that will smother his plans.

Faith causes fiery arrows to fizzle. As you move forward, you'll sense a holy confidence swelling, a bold courage growing, and a hopeful anticipation rising in you—pushing back the obstacles that once overwhelmed you.

Recall a time when you sensed your confidence growing and the fiery arrows fading as you walked by faith.

The enemy knows the power of faith, too. And that's why he's working overtime to keep you too busy or too afraid to take the risk. The only way strongholds can be broken in your life is if you push past any "internal fires," refuse to let them distract you any longer, and get that shield of faith in position.

Think back to the issue you wrote down at the end of Day 1—the clear directive you know you're being told to follow. What is one step you can take in the direction of obedience before this week is over that will be the "proof" of your commitment?

Who can you employ to keep you accountable in this?

As you move forward in obedience, come back here to keep notes on how you sense the fiery darts of the enemy fizzling more and more each day.

THE TURTLE FORMATION

Roman soldiers, when advancing in battle, would naturally hold their shields in front of them. But when the enemy was launching the flaming missiles, the soldiers would use them more strategically.

They would dip their shields in water, then huddle together in a group, hoisting the shields overhead. Strategically placed hooks on the sides of the shields would allow them to be linked together. When formed into a unit like this, their water-soaked shields would create a damp, dense shell of protection above them—called the turtle formation. And because the shields actually had "a gap between the layers ... flaming arrows could penetrate far enough into the shield to be quickly extinguished."[4]

That's right. The shield not only deflected the arrows; it also extinguished them.

Consider the Roman army's turtle formation in light of Paul's emphasis on our relationships with one another in the body of Christ. What does this say about how we should concern ourselves with building up the faith of others? And how should active faith strengthen the broader community of Christ? Prepare to discuss this with your group. See Ecclesiastes 4:9-12 for inspiration in your discussion.

Hebrews 11 has long been described as the Hall of Faith. Look at each of the following people, and write down any observations you find interesting about how they exhibited active faith.

- **Noah (v. 7)**

- **Abraham (vv. 8-10)**

- **Sarah (vv. 11-12)**

- **Moses (vv. 24-26)**

> **FAITH DOESN'T JUST DEFLECT THE ENEMY'S ACCUSATIONS; IT EXTINGUISHES THEM.**
> *#ArmorOfGodStudy*

Two-thirds of a scutum would cover one whole soldier and one-third of another. So when shields were interlocked, gaps in the formation were eradicated.

How did these actions "extinguish" anything that could have crippled them?

What could have been the tragic effects if they'd chosen not to move forward in faith? How would it have affected their families for generations to come?

Why would this have been to the enemy's advantage?

Which of these people and stories do you most personally relate to? Any of them? If so, what makes their situation similar to yours?

Each of these individuals had to make the difficult choice: succumb to what they could see, or trust God with what they couldn't. Only acting in faith puts you in the "turtle formation" and extinguishes the darts that the enemy assigns for your life. So if you want to see insecurity quelled, doubts suppressed, fears quieted, hate overpowered, or intimidation assuaged, move forward in obedience. In faith.

This means choosing to live with an unwavering confidence in God and His promises to you. It's walking forward in accordance with truth as revealed in His Word. Faith is pushing past the fear or doubts that may seek to paralyze you in insecurity, and choosing instead to follow God where He is leading, trusting that He will take care of the rest.

Today, your "actionable intel" should literally be an action plan. What is God asking you to do? Do it! In faith, believing God's "turtle shell" of protection that will destroy the enemy's crafty attempts to ruin us.

Actionable Intel...

DAY 3
IN GOOD FAITH

After sixteen years of marriage, Jerry and I decided to build a house. We looked forward to the process and were excited to see it begin.

We had our eye on a specific builder that we'd been hoping would take on our project. He was extremely reputable, having built homes in and around the Dallas/Fort Worth area for decades; well-known and respected for his commitment to quality, excellence, and integrity. On top of that, he'd been personal friends with my father for nearly two decades. So we knew we could trust him.

We set up our first meeting with both him and the architect who was going to help us craft a design that would work for our family. But before that first meeting, he emailed us a copy of a contract he wanted us to sign, spelling out the terms of our initial agreement to build with his company. But the contract required more than just our signature. A hefty deposit, referred to as earnest money or a "good faith" payment, would also be necessary in order to move forward. Jerry and I signed the paper and wrote the check to present at our first meeting.

From the illustration above, answer the following questions:
What is the difference in commitment level between signing a contract and writing the check to seal it?

In addition to the commitment level, what is the difference in risk and sacrifice involved in signing the contract versus writing the check?

How might this correlate to the difference between belief and faith?

What did our willingness to write that check reveal about our desire to build a house?

What did it reveal about how we felt about the builder?

Writing the check required a deeper commitment level than simply signing the contract. And it put us in a much more risky position than if we'd only signed the document. But Jerry and I were willing to do both because we wanted to express our full dedication to the process.

Writing that check did something more, however. It also made an important statement. It communicated that we believed the builder was trustworthy enough to follow through on the deal. His faithfulness over the course of many decades, as well as his strong character and our own personal knowledge of his integrity, gave us the solid foundation we needed for feeling confident about making this decision. He had proven himself so consistently that we knew he was worth the risk.

Taking up the shield of faith is like writing a check of trust to God. It is proof that you trust Him like you say you do. Yes, faith usually involves sacrifice because it likely involves some level of risk on your part. But it's a risk worth taking if the One on whom you're depending has proven Himself dependable, time and time again, from one generation to the next. Your God is faithful—"faith-full"—and this is why you can live a faith-filled life.

In Day 2, you looked at four people mentioned in Hebrews 11. Flip back and choose one, and then take a few moments to consider what might have been the sacrifice involved in their choice to obey God. Record your findings.

Carefully consider and record what it would cost you to walk in faith in the area of your life that you've been considering this week.

How has the cost kept you from following through?

> ## BECAUSE HE IS FAITH-FULL, I CAN BE FAITH-FILLED.
> *#ArmorOfGodStudy*

FAITHFUL

It's possible, in reading Paul's description of faith as a protector against the enemy's attacks, to misconstrue his connotation—to think that we humans somehow have the power to protect ourselves if we have the right amount of faith. But two things are important to consider here. First, faith does not control God. It doesn't make God do something. A better understanding of what happens when we exhibit faith is that it gives us access to what God has already intended to do for us.

Paul made this point in Ephesians 2, for example, in talking about the role of faith in our salvation. God is the One who graciously made salvation available to us; faith is simply what allows us to gain access to it. Our faith doesn't manufacture our salvation. Salvation is a gift, but faith allows us to receive that gift by grace.

Secondly, what we mean by "having faith" actually says far less about us and a lot more about God. Faith does not focus on the quality or quantity of human belief. It focuses on how trustworthy, true, and loyal the object of that belief has proven Himself to be.

How have you seen God prove Himself trustworthy, true, or loyal in your life or the life of someone you know? Write your thoughts below and prepare to share with your group when you meet again.

Read Luke 17:5-6 in the margin. Underline what the disciples asked for. Circle Jesus' response.

In Luke 17, when the apostles requested that Jesus give them more faith, Jesus had been talking to them about the importance of forgiving those who'd hurt or offended them—how they should forgive not grudgingly or sparingly, but continuously and lavishly. The disciples felt so ill-equipped to obey this task (as we all do at one point or another) that they asked for more faith to help them do it.

For by grace you have been saved through faith; and that not of yourselves, it is the gift of God (Eph. 2:8).

The apostles said to the Lord, "Increase our faith." "If you have faith the size of a mustard seed," the Lord said, "you can say to this mulberry tree, 'Be uprooted and planted in the sea,' and it will obey you" (Luke 17:5-6, CSB).

Jesus' response to the disciples is telling. He said in no uncertain terms that someone with even a tiny bit of faith—the size of a small seed—has enough to live a faith-filled life. And the reason is clear: a little faith is all you need when it's firmly planted in the right Person. "Good faith" isn't a certain size or strength; it's simply faith that's directed at and rooted in a good God.

GOOD FAITH IS ROOTED IN A GOOD GOD.
#ArmorOfGodStudy

Have you ever felt the need for "more faith" to do what you feel God is asking you to do? What were the circumstances surrounding this?

Look up passages like Matthew 6:30; 8:26; and 16:8, where Jesus quantifies someone's faith as "little." In these cases the size of their faith correlates directly to their view of Jesus. Jesus is calling the disciples to a clearer understanding of His ability and His care for them. He is not challenging them to focus on faith; He is telling them to focus on Him.

Listen to me carefully. If you are struggling to move forward in obedience to God, you do not need bigger faith. You just need to realize how big your God is. The more faithful and strong you believe Him to be, the more willing you'll be to depend on Him. Your level of faith will always be tied to your perception of God. If your perception of Him is faulty, your faith will be faulty. If your perception of Him is on point, your faith will be too. You don't need more faith; you need a more comprehensive and accurate view of the faithfulness of your God.

In regard to the step of faith you've been personally considering throughout this week of study, what do your actions (your obedience or lack thereof) say about how you truly feel about the faithfulness and integrity of God?

☐ **I trust that God is powerful and strong and that He loves me and will take good care of me.**

☐ **I believe God is powerful and strong, yes, but I question His love and desire to care for me.**

☐ **I guess I don't really believe He's all-powerful. I'm not sure He'll protect me.**

Choose one Old Testament verse and one New Testament verse from the options below. Read them slowly and prayerfully. Write down the words or phrases from each verse that speaks to you the most convincingly about the faithfulness of God. Consider including phrases from these verses in your prayer strategy this week so you can consistently be reminded of how trustworthy your God is.

Old Testament	New Testament
Deuteronomy 7:9	2 Thessalonians 3:3
Psalm 36:5	1 Corinthians 10:13
Isaiah 25:1	2 Timothy 2:13

Our action or inaction is a litmus test that gives us an accurate reading of what we believe to be true about God. We may feel like we have very little faith, and yet still be people of strong faith because we choose to move forward despite what we feel. Conversely, we can be people who claim to have strong faith, ready to go on an adventure with God—and yet when He actually calls us to do it, we refuse either because we succumb to fear and doubt or we're distracted by life circumstances that seem more pressing and urgent. So we can never detect our level of faith (or the faith of another, for that matter) by how we feel, only by what we're willing to do in obedience to God.

As you proactively remind yourself of how faithful and reliable your God truly is, you'll become more willing—even excited—about actually relying on Him. Your shield of faith works because it is directly connected to the faithfulness of your God.

> For the LORD is good; his steadfast love endures forever, and his faithfulness to all generations (Ps. 100:5, ESV).

Actionable Intel...

A FIRM FOUNDATION

Earlier this week, we defined *faith* with this simple meaning: acting like God is telling the truth.

Truth. This is the hinge upon which the entire issue of faith-filled living rests. If you don't know the truth, you can never really know how to act in conjunction with it. So the truth of God's character and His Word provides the framework that allows our faith to flourish and thrive.

Why do you think the connection between truth and faith is critical?

Recall a time when you or someone you know has acted without having a firm foundation of truth. What was the outcome of the situation?

The truth of God is what makes having faith in God worth it. Without truth, we have nothing solid to hang our shield of faith on. So knowing the truth of God and the truth about God as revealed in His Word is critical if we want to live out our faith responsibly, if we want to experience the benefits of being protected by our shields.

We studied Luke 5:1-7,11 in this week's group discussion—the story about Jesus telling Simon to go back out and try casting his fishing nets one more time. Let's look at it more closely here.

Open your Bible to this passage and read the story from beginning to end. Then answer the following questions:

After a discouraging night of fishing, what was Simon doing at the end of verse 2 that would have made Jesus' instructions even more difficult to follow later on?

Think about the connection between truth and faith. What do you think is the importance of this statement in verse 4: "When He [Jesus] had finished speaking, He said to Simon ..." [emphasis mine]?

How does Simon's response to Jesus in verse 5 reveal some of the "fiery darts" he might have been dealing with?

What did Simon say (also in v. 5) that reveals the moment he employed the shield of faith?

How did Simon and his companions respond to what happened (v. 11)?

Circle any of the questions that hit close to home for you personally. Below, record the ways these details connect to something you are facing right now.

What is God asking you to do in response to what you've seen in Simon's example?

Once Simon heard Jesus' command, he no longer allowed his experience as a fisherman or his disappointment from the night before to keep him from moving forward. He trusted Jesus and His word more than he trusted even his own perceptions, skills, and feelings. He didn't allow himself to be disabled by doubt or even hampered by exhaustion. He'd heard the truth—the word of God—and believed. To prove it, he went where he'd been asked to go despite how he felt. Jesus had spoken—and that was enough. Enough to make him willing to dirty up nets he'd just cleaned. Enough to row his boat from the security of shore to the deep waters outside of his comfort zone. And, ultimately, enough to follow

Jesus from that point forward, wherever He might lead, for the rest of his days. Hearing God and knowing His truth matters.

HEARING GOD

Any discussion on faith would be incomplete without highlighting the critical importance of hearing the voice of God clearly and accurately. If we aren't careful, faith can easily turn to foolishness—imprudent, impulsive, even reckless and dangerous, behavior done in the name of faith. But true faith must always be built squarely on the foundation of God's written Word as His Spirit leads you to apply it to your life.

My sheep hear My voice, and I know them, and they follow Me (John 10:27).

How would you describe the difference between faith and foolishness?

What keeps someone from crossing the boundary between the two?

God has already made Himself clear on many things in His unchanging Word. But when seeking clarity on the finer details of our personal lives—on whether or not, like Simon, to launch out into deep waters—God's Spirit will convict (John 16:8), teach (1 John 2:27), guide (John 16:13), and lead (Matt. 4:1). He may do it with biblical principles, or perhaps through the added confirmation of godly counsel and the ordering of circumstances around you.

As believers, we have the privilege of knowing His direction for us as we prayerfully seek it. He will be faithful to show us the truth, to give us His direction for the next step we are supposed to take. In fact, being confident and affirmed in that next step is critical in order to help us stay balanced as we pursue a lifestyle protected by the shield of faith.

Look up the following verses that reveal God's word in a particular area of life. Draw a line to connect the reference with the corresponding truth, promise, or directive.

Deuteronomy 31:6	Forgive
Philippians 4:6	Watch what you say and how you say it
Romans 13:1-2	Flee from sexual immorality
2 Corinthians 6:14	Do not be bound in a relationship with an unbeliever
Ephesians 4:29	Be grateful instead of anxious
2 Corinthians 2:7	God will never leave your side
Malachi 3:10	Go to church
1 Corinthians 6:18	Submit to and respect authority
Hebrews 10:25	Tithe

Circle any of the issues in the chart above that might apply to an area of your life now or even in a past season. Answer the following questions:

Have you responded in obedience to the truth revealed in the Bible? Why or why not?

Have you in any way allowed your feelings to override your commitment to obey?

If so, what has been the outcome of following your feelings?

Once you clearly know the truth of God or the promise of God in regards to a matter, it's time to move forward in a way that's congruent with it. Listen carefully—your feelings can never be the final determining factor for your actions. Feelings change and are subject to external stimuli. Actions done in faith must be anchored in something more solid and fixed. Your enemy is always hoping you'll be swayed by how you feel instead of acting in conjunction with the steady, sacred truth that you know. That's why he works overtime to make you feel insecure, unloved, incapable, or (and this seems to be his favorite ploy) afraid. He hopes you'll trust those feelings and be directed by them, instead of following the truth of God's Word.

And, speaking of fear ...

THE FEAR FACTOR

God has not given us a spirit of fear, but of power and of love and of a sound mind (2 Tim. 1:7, NKJV).

Fear is one of the enemy's most useful deterrents to faith-filled living. Fear will make you want to drop your shield and run away. In fact, fear is one of Satan's primary schemes for crippling and paralyzing God's people. I'm not talking about legitimate concern or the protective warnings of wisdom and godly counsel. I'm talking about fear. Incessant worry. Up-all-night anxiety. Worst-case scenarios becoming the only probabilities you can think about.

This issue of fear is so well-known and important to God that more than three hundred times in Scripture, He tells His people—in one form or another—not to be afraid. "Fear not." "Be ye not afraid." "Do not fear." Look it up. It's everywhere. You know those times when you're searching high and low for just one verse to tell you what God wants you to do? Well, here's three hundred of them. And they're all saying the same thing: "Don't be afraid."

Write down any part that fear is playing in keeping you from walking by faith in your life right now.

Is there any way you are nurturing or encouraging this fear in your life instead of fighting to overcome it?

Tomorrow, you and I are going to launch into writing our prayer strategies for this week. But I wanted you to zero in ahead of time on this area of fear. To call it out and name it for what it truly is—a ploy by the enemy to keep you from walking in truth. Wherever there is fear, you can always be assured the enemy is nearby, strategically seeking to stall you or paralyze you from what he knows is God's best for you.

But this week, his reign of terror is coming to an end. Because now you know the truth. We've called his bluff. Our God is true and worth following. He is always there—far outranking Satan in strength—to hear our troubled prayers, reaffirm His fearless promises, and deliver the next bit of lamplight we need for walking steadily in His direction.

Shields up, soldiers. We're walking by faith.

Actionable Intel...

DAY 5
STRATEGY SESSION

There is a bridge near our home that crosses a deep ravine. It looks a tad mousey and unstable. Most anytime new visitors drive up, they will stop their car at the foot of the bridge, unsure whether to risk going across. But not me. I never worry about whether or not to cross the bridge. Whenever I drive up to it, I immediately and easily pull my car down the path without any reservations. My reason is simple: our ministry office building is on the other side of that bridge, and UPS® regularly makes deliveries. So since I've seen two-ton trucks safely traverse it time and time again, I know it can carry the load of my little four-door sedan without any problems. The daily integrity of the bridge has earned my trust and has made me feel confident to take the risk of going across myself.

This week you've been thinking about whether or not to "cross the bridge"—whether to take the risk of faith and follow God where He is leading in particular areas of your life. As you close this week by gathering your Actionable Intel and preparing your prayer strategy, make it your goal to accentuate the faithfulness of God.

Remind yourself that He has carried the weight of a covenant with His people across generations. His loyalty, integrity, and faithfulness are unmatched.

Write down His promises and declarations of faithfulness to you as a part of your prayers. One mention of them will not only bolster your own confidence, but will extinguish some arrows aimed in your direction. Let the devil hear you saying ...

> *Know therefore that the LORD your God is God; he is the faithful God, keeping his covenant of love to a thousand generations of those who love him and keep his commands (Deut. 7:9, NIV).*

And …

> We know that in all things God works for the good of those who love him, who have been called according to his purpose (Rom. 8:28, NIV).

And …

> Let us hold unswervingly to the hope we profess, for he who promised is faithful (Heb. 10:23, NIV).

And …

> The LORD is on my side; I will not fear (Ps. 118:6, ESV).

And every time you vocalize the prayer that you are about to write, remind yourself and declare to the devil that your God is a bridge worth crossing because He'll never let you down.

Not ever.

He is always worth the risk.

THE HELMET OF
SALVATION

Imagine you were meeting your Bible study group for the first time. How would you introduce yourself? What would you reveal about your identity, about what you enjoy or how you think about yourself?

Your identity isn't just your name and age, the sports you play or the things you're good at. It's also your character and personality, the unique way that you think about yourself and the world. Your identity, simply put, is who you are.

Your identity is a vital part of understanding the piece of armor you'll study this week: the helmet of salvation.

Read Ephesians 6:10-19. As you read, underline the three pieces of armor that should be part of your uniform. Circle the three pieces we're told to pick up or put on.

Most people don't realize that salvation has two facets: it rescues but then it frees. Salvation isn't just about being rescued or redeemed; it's also about being set free. A synonym for the word salvation is liberation.

Read Galatians 5:1. Take note of the words that point to the idea of freedom or liberation.

Why do you think it's important to understand that salvation is about more than being redeemed and spending eternity with Jesus, but also that it empowers up to live in freedom on earth?

So it turns out salvation is not just about redemption. It is also a defensive protective device as well. It isn't only about giving you a ticket to eternity. It is about so much more. It's not just about saving you from hell. It's about allowing you to live victoriously while you're right here on Earth.

Listen, if all you do is receive salvation, and I pray that you have, but if that's all that you do, you're going to miss out on so much of what salvation was meant to give you. It was meant to reorient your entire identity and implement an entire new way of thinking into your life. Salvation was not only meant to be received; it was meant to be applied. We're supposed to walk in the liberation we have been given because we have been redeemed by the Cross of Calvary.

Have you ever gotten a song stuck in your head? What song was it? How long did it last?

What about an idea? Have you ever gotten an idea about yourself, someone else, or even God that you later discovered wasn't true? What did the experience teach you about yourself? About God?

The enemy is after your mind. He wants to dig deeply into your thought patterns, so he can keep your thoughts far away from God. He wants to keep you from considering God's thoughts, His ways, His voice, and His wisdom, so you can't figure out what God would have you do in any scenario in your life. He's working hard to ruin your thought life, so he can ruin your behaviors.

Read 2 Corinthians 10:3-5. Circle the word strongholds (Some translations may say fortresses.). Underline any other military terms you see in these verses. What does the strong, militaristic language Paul used teach you about the war we as believers are waging against the enemy?

Work together to create a definition for *stronghold* based on the verses you just read. Write it below, then discuss.

We are fighting a war against Satan, and we need the helmet of salvation to win. But just like the shield of faith, we have to do more than receive it. We have to apply salvation to our daily lives. If you're a believer in Jesus Christ, you have salvation. Now you've got to use it. It is designed to protect you in all of the places, namely your mind where the enemy is most after you. It's time to put the helmet on.

Turn to the inside back cover and examine the soldier's helmet. How would you describe it? What kind of protection might this piece of armor provide?

Scholars say that about a decade before Paul wrote this letter, the Roman soldier's helmet was redesigned. They added pieces so the back of the neck would also be covered and incorporated some trim along the sides so that the face would have more coverage as well. The additions allowed the helmet to provide more comprehensive, thorough coverage to the soldier's head and face. The redesigned helmet simply provided better protection than the earlier design had.

For Paul, that was a perfect illustration for the concept of salvation. Salvation gives you comprehensive coverage. It provides everything you need to remain safeguarded. Paul wanted us to understand that our salvation wasn't just about victory some day in the future when we meet Jesus. Instead, it's designed to allow us to walk in victory every day of our lives.

Read Proverbs 23:7 aloud. What does this verse teach us about the importance of our thoughts? Explain.

The New King James version puts it this way: "For as he thinks within himself, so he is." We know that our physical brains control all the functions of our bodies. The signals our brains send regulate our hearts, breathing, and more. That means if your brain is impaired, even in the smallest way, it will affect, impair, or incapacitate some part of your body. The same is true spiritually. Whatever we let control our minds, the thought patterns we let run wild—whether true or not—direct our actions and behaviors.

Salvation is about your identity. It's who you are in Christ. Read the underlined statement aloud, then write it below.

Now, read Ephesians 1:3-17 aloud. As you read, take note of every word or phrase that describes who you are—your identity—as a believer in Christ.

Blessed. Chosen. Holy. Blameless. Redeemed. Raised up. Seated in the heavenly places. Adopted. Forgiven. All of these and more describe who you are as a child of God. Verse 3 says that God Himself is blessed, which means that as His child, you are too. You can walk with your chin up, focusing your eyes on Him, seeking Him, growing in Him,

100 percent confident that He is a father who seeks to bless you with all the spiritual blessings you will ever need. In Jesus, He has already made them available to you.

Read Ephesians 1:18-22, finishing out the chapter. What did Paul pray for believers in verse 18? Why?

Your eyes need to be continually opened to who you are in Christ rather than who the world says you are. When you put on the helmet of the salvation, you remind yourself whose child you are. Maybe you've been told your entire life that you're worthless, that you'll never amount to anything. Perhaps the people you've loved have undervalued you, walked all over you like a doormat. Whatever it is you have been told about yourself, put on the helmet of salvation by rehearsing your identity in Christ.

Sometimes the greatest miracles God works are not in our circumstances but in our minds. Salvation does more than rescue us from a state of danger; it makes us whole. It restores us. Who you are in Christ guards and protects you against the schemes of the enemy.

So, how do we fight back? Read Romans 12:1-2. Write it in your own words below.

Our minds are renewed through the Word of God. It's alive—living and active and sharper than any two-edged sword. Strongholds are torn down by the Word of God. Toxic thinking is dismantled. When you and I apply our identity in Christ to our everyday lives, we reshape and rewire our brains.

What toxic thought patterns or beliefs have you allowed to shape how you think about yourself? How will you put on the helmet of salvation to fight those this week?

What verses or truths from Scripture will you focus on to combat those lies of the enemy?

This week, let your mind be renewed. Revel in and meditate on your identity in Christ. Retrain your thinking so that it lines up with the Word of God. Never forget who you are because of whose you are. You are valuable, accepted, loved, forgiven, redeemed, and liberated. You are His child. Put on the helmet of salvation.

DAY 1

SO GREAT A SALVATION

My second son, JC, hurt himself pretty badly a few years ago. He was riding his bike downhill, trailing too closely behind his cousin Jessie. As their velocity picked up, Jessie decided to apply his brakes without warning. And because JC was so close behind, he slammed on his brakes—hard. Hard enough to send him flying over the top of his handlebars and onto the concrete road.

He emerged with a fractured wrist and a horribly skinned knee—the kind of wound that requires a special ointment, applied every day to fight off infection. It stung just a bit when we applied it. He didn't like the process too much. But we did it anyway.

Because just having the right medicine isn't enough if he wants all the benefits of it. The only way to receive its intended healing effect is to apply the medicine—not every now and then, but every single day.

The best you can, try to define and describe *salvation*. What does it mean and what does it accomplish for us?

START TO FINISH

Having something does not ensure that the recipient will experience the benefits that only using it can yield. This distinction is critical to keep in mind as Paul introduces the next piece of spiritual armor.

Write just the first part of Ephesians 6:17 in the space below.

Turn to the inside back cover and take a look at a traditional Roman soldier's helmet. Write the corresponding spiritual principle next to it.

Why do you think Paul chose to associate salvation with this particular piece of armor?

In what sense do you think our salvation can act as a protective measure for our minds? Explain.

The salvation experience is often reduced to something that only affects a person's eternal destiny—heaven or hell. And to be clear, it does affect the outcome of eternity, which gives us incredible hope. In fact, part of what it means to wear the helmet of salvation is to live every day in light of eternity and the promised future that we have. Doing so will change the way we live in the present.

First Thessalonians 5:8 calls the helmet "the hope of salvation." Discuss with your group the ways that our ultimate salvation in Christ gives us hope and confidence even while living through the trials and difficulties of earth. How does it inform our choices, feelings, and actions? For more, see Romans 8:23-24.

> *The helmet of salvation is likely taken directly from the description of the Divine Warrior in Isaiah 59:17— "He put ... a helmet of salvation on His head."*

While the future implications of our salvation are critical and give us astounding hope, this is not all that it offers. If salvation was only meant to give us a ticket to eternity, what good would it do us now? Do we just sit around waiting, living out our days until the Lord returns or we go to heaven, whichever comes first?

No, salvation—yours and mine—was meant to come with more than future benefits. It was also supposed to exert a clear impact on our present, daily lives. But we'll only experience that impact to the extent that we apply the benefits of salvation to our everyday lives.

Receiving salvation is not the same as applying salvation. The first redeems us; the second restores, protects, and shields us daily from the attacks of the enemy.

So let's look at several passages that will help us understand salvation more fully.

Read Romans 5:9-10 in the margin. Read it through two times very slowly, aloud if you'd like.

How do these verses help you to better understand both receiving and applying salvation? Record your thoughts below.

We looked at James 1:21 in Week 3. Consider the second half of this verse again in light of what we're studying today. As you do, remember that the Book of James, like Romans, was written to people who were already believers. Record the multi-layered effectiveness of salvation expressed in this verse.

These passages give us a clear perspective of the present-tense effectiveness of salvation. First, Christ's death justifies us by declaring us "righteous by his blood" (Rom. 5:9, CSB). *Justification* is a legal term signifying acquittal. It means we're released from having to pay the debt we owe for our sin.

But our salvation doesn't stop at the foot of the cross. If you're amazed at what His death accomplished, imagine how much more is accomplished through "his life" (Rom. 5:10). The fact that He lives means our salvation flows into the everyday experiences where we live. As James 1:21 says, our "souls" are saved daily and progressively through the Spirit and the Word of God. This is sanctification, and it is how we are able to experience the abundant life that Christ came to give all who believe in His name.

From Week 3 of our study, do you recall what sanctification is? Write a definition in your own words below.

Describe the difference between sanctification and justification.

How does the sanctification process affect the mind?

Salvation is not just a past-tense event (justification) with future-tense implications. As we live underneath its blessing, we enjoy a vibrant, living, daily reality in the present (sanctification). And this is not just a one-time occurrence. Sanctification is a process by which we are continually delivered from the wrath of God on earth, fortified against the enemy's attacks, and molded into the image of Christ as our minds are renewed.

Now we're starting to understand what it means to put on salvation like a helmet.

Go back and look at the verses you've been studying today from Romans 5 and James 1. Underline any words or phrases that relate to justification. Circle any that convey sanctification.

Do you usually tend to think of salvation only in terms of what it meant for your past (justification) or your future (glorification)? Or do you also think of it in terms of daily living (sanctification)? Explain your answer.

What does applying salvation to your daily life actually look like? What practical benefits do you see filtering into your experience? Prepare to discuss this with your group.

RESCUED AND RESTORED

Look at this telling definition of salvation from the *Lexham Theological Wordbook*: Salvation is the rescue from a state of danger and the "restoration to wholeness and prosperity."[1] This reference goes on to explain that in the Bible, when the word *saved* is used, even in referencing one nation being saved from foreign enemies, it doesn't just involve them escaping death but also entering into a state of health, wholeness, victory, and safety. Our God's salvation involves the well-being of the whole person—not just rescuing them but even reversing negative circumstances.

Consider the two highlighted words in the previous paragraph. In what ways have you seen or experienced both? List any examples you can think of.

1. Salvation's rescuing power

2. Salvation's restoring power

> **SALVATION IS NOT JUST A PAST EVENT; IT IS ALSO A PRESENT REALITY.**
> #ArmorOfGodStudy

If our salvation offered no more than redemption from our sins and escape from its penalty, you know what? That would be enough to celebrate for the rest of our days. Because the fact is that there is a profound hope that overwhelms us just knowing this world is not our home. But God in His astounding graciousness has designed salvation to offer so much more. And as we begin to unpack it in the days ahead, you'll see your salvation becoming a defensive, protective device that covers you, shields you, and protects you against the schemes of the devil. It enables you to lead whole, healthy lives not fractured by the enemy's deceptive strategies.

This is what the devil doesn't want you to know. Because as long as you don't apply salvation to your life, you'll still be vulnerable to his attacks every day for the rest of your life, even if you're saved.

So this week we are going to explore what the Bible means when it says to "work out your salvation" (Phil. 2:12)—to put it on as a helmet of protection for your life. End today's lesson by not only writing your Actionable Intel, but also thanking the Lord for the fullness of your salvation—the power to rescue you and restore you. Then determine to "be sober, having put on the breastplate of faith and love, and as a helmet, the hope of salvation" (1 Thess. 5:8). Meet you back here tomorrow to set it solidly in place.

Actionable Intel...

DAY 2
THE INHERITANCE

My family and I enjoy going to camp in the summertime. We've made fond memories at several of them over the years. We love the outdoor activities, the atmosphere of excitement, and the emphasis on cultivating spiritual development. I've also long admired the counselors and camp workers who make places like these flourish year after year. They work tirelessly, day in and day out, in piping hot summer temperatures. And let's just say, they mostly do it for the love. I know for sure they don't do it for the money.

Which is why I was pretty intrigued one summer when I went to visit a couple who'd worked in one of these camp settings for more than a decade. Their home was absolutely stunning. It had beautiful architectural detail, spacious rooms, positioned right on the banks of a placid, gorgeous lake. Clearly it was worth a pretty penny. Beautiful.

But ...

They must've seen that look enough times before to know what I was thinking. I was right, they told me: the salary they made at the camp they loved so much wasn't enough—would never be enough—to put a house like this one within their budget. But they'd been able to afford it anyway. How? Because one of their parents had left them a hefty inheritance. So even though they were still devoting their time and energy to their job, they were able to function in a way that was beyond the limitations of what it could provide. They didn't live based on their modest yearly salary; they lived based on their inheritance—a substantial gift from someone who loved them.

What would you change about your current lifestyle if you received a substantial financial inheritance in the next 24 hours?

In Him also we have obtained an inheritance, having been predestined according to His purpose who works all things after the counsel of His will, to the end that we who were the first to hope in Christ would be to the praise of His glory (Eph. 1:10b-12).

Read Ephesians 1:10b-12 in the margin. Underline the words or phrases that stand out most to you.
According to this verse:
• What have we received?

• How did we come to be recipients of it?

• What should be the outcome of us having it?

What would change about the status of your current mental, emotional, or spiritual well-being if you found out about a substantial spiritual inheritance that belonged to you?

AN HEIR OF GOD

When the apostle Paul opened his letter to the Ephesians, he spent the majority of this first portion accentuating the grand benefits inherent in salvation. But the depths of God's love in choosing us, adopting us, bestowing grace upon us, and redeeming us are only the beginning of what our relationship with Christ offers. We've also received a vast, boundless, lavish inheritance—one that we did not earn and do not deserve. And Paul wanted to make sure we never forget it. Because if we do, we'll likely live a lifestyle well below our actual means. We'll live within the meager restraints of our earthly resources instead of cashing in on the wealth of our Father.

Put an asterisk beside three of the Scriptures from the Digging Deeper article on page 182 that speak most to you right now in your life.

Turn to Digging Deeper 5 which lists some of your inheritance and identity in Christ (page 182). Read it. Rehearse it. Savor it.

Understand that living in light of this salvation inheritance enables you to not only stop living below your spiritual station in life, but it also protects your mind against the enemy's attempts to cripple your thinking, to convince you that you are worth less than you really are. The ripple effect of this protection will be a change in your mind-set, lifestyle, and the choices you make. All of that will now be based on your wealthy spiritual income status. And this new way of looking at things will begin changing the outcome of the battles you face against the enemy, deflecting all his attempts at thwarting you from reaching your destiny.

Romans 8:17 echoes the inheritance principle and your relationship to it. Turn to this passage in your Bible and write it word-for-word in the space provided.

Consider the phrase "heirs of God" from Romans 8:17. What should your perspective be about the quality and quantity of this inheritance you've received, since your benefactor is God Himself?

PUT THAT HELMET ON

A Roman soldier's <u>helmet</u> was basically a skullcap made of iron, typically covered with bronze. Its primary function was to protect the soldier's skull and brain from the swing of the "broadsword"—a three- to four-foot long sword with a massive handle that needed to be cradled by two hands to hit its target. (Yikes.) One strategically aimed blow could completely crush the soldier's skull, incapacitating him in a split second.

The helmet of the Roman legionary was called a galea.[2]

Over time, the soldier's helmet was redesigned to be even more comprehensive in its coverage. Pieces were added, including a flared neck guard and hinged cheek guards. It protected not only the head but also the neck and shoulders.[3] "When the helmet was strapped in place, it exposed little besides the eyes, nose, and mouth."[4]

Comprehensive coverage. Put on. Placed on one of the most vital parts of the believer's spiritual livelihood. This helmet of salvation, positioned to a snug fit, is representative of the things that are ours "in Him"—our inheritance in Christ. Choosing not to wear it means leaving our mind exposed, unprotected, like people who don't even own a helmet.

From the following verses, what is the importance of the mind to the believer's ability to function in health and victory?

- Isaiah 26:3-4

- Romans 8:6-7

- 1 Corinthians 14:20

- Hebrews 8:10

- 1 Peter 1:13-16

Considering the physical brain can help explain the importance and function of the mind. The significant role your brain plays is profound. Every single function of your body—whether just a small movement of your pinkie finger to operating a car or running a marathon—is attached to the signals and impulses your brain sends. If your brain is impaired, your body will also be impaired, no matter how healthy the individual parts of your body may be.

And what the brain is to the body, your mind is to your soul. It is the spiritual expression of your brain. The control center. If your mind doesn't send out healthy impulses, your soul will not respond in healthy ways. This is why the enemy works so diligently to cripple you through negative thoughts and unhealthy patterns of imagination.

Recall and list the four parts that make up the human soul. (Reference page 73 for a refresher if you need to.)

1.

2.

3.

4.

Look at the following chart that exposes some of Satan's most common attacks against the minds of Christians. Beside each one, write down one or two words that describe the negative ripple effects—both emotional and behavioral—that someone might experience as a result of nursing these thought patterns:

THINK	FEEL	ACT
I am unworthy.		
I am unloved.		
I am incapable.		
I am undesirable.		
I am unforgivable.		
I am unknown.		
My life is insignificant.		
I am a mistake.		
I can lose my salvation.		
Other		

Which of these thought patterns best describes something you've personally struggled with?

Do you struggle with an uncontrolled fantasy life? Describe those runaway thoughts.

A good person produces good out of the good stored up in his heart. An evil person produces evil out of the evil stored up in his heart, for his mouth speaks from the overflow of the heart (Luke 6:45, CSB).

How have your emotional health and behavioral choices reflected any patterns of defective thinking that the enemy has suggested and that you have perpetrated?

The health of your mind has everything to do with your overall ability to function properly, both emotionally and behaviorally. If your mind's thought processes are unhealthy and toxic, your emotions and actions will expose it.

As if that's not enough, poisonous thinking will also cripple your ability to clearly detect the leading of God's Spirit. As an heir, you're meant to know and discern His will, to hear His guiding voice behind you. But when your mind isn't thinking like someone who wears salvation, your conscience (which is part of your soul, remember?) fails to turn in the direction of the Spirit's conviction. The enemy's lies, when believed, short-circuit and distort your ability to hear God's voice clearly and respond accordingly.

But you are an heir, OK? You don't need to live from such a limited perspective of scarcity and lack—unprotected, unshielded, vulnerable to assault. Your inheritance, so full and rich and robust and plentiful, was bestowed upon you by Someone who died on your behalf nearly 2,000 years ago. So while you still go about your regular life with your regular life circumstances, you aren't limited by their meager restraints. Your lifestyle should reflect your true inheritance which will enable you to live a spiritual life of lavish abundance and grace. It is a helmet of protection for your head, for your mind. Put it on and you'll begin to see a raise in your standard of living right away.

Actionable Intel...

DAY 3
THE BENEFITS PACKAGE

Earlier in our study I mentioned that Roman soldiers of Paul's day needed to buy their own equipment. Their suit of armor was not government-issued until much later. Only those who were wealthy enough to buy their own helmets were able to secure themselves in the protection this critical piece of armor provides. So the poor went into battle unprotected. Their helmet, unlike ours, wasn't free of charge.

What adjectives would you use to describe how a soldier might feel going into battle without a helmet?

For by grace you have been saved through faith; and that not of yourselves, it is the gift of God (Eph. 2:8).

Having a helmet is a confidence-builder. It provides the security of protection in the midst of heated battle. The good news for us is that we never have a reason to be without it. The price for our helmet has been <u>paid in full</u> by our Savior. What a shame if we ever go into battle again without taking full advantage of it—and of the full benefits package that comes with it.

The following is a list of the negative and toxic thoughts we began considering on Day 2. Turn to Ephesians 1:4-14 and 2:1-10, where Paul outlined the benefits of our salvation. Search these verses for truths that combat each of the lies of the enemy. Write some key words beside each one in the space below. I've given you an example. And, by the way, one truth may apply to several of these thoughts.

LIES	TRUTHS
I am unworthy.	Holy. Blameless. (1:4)
I am unloved.	
I am incapable.	
I am undesirable.	
I am unforgivable.	
I am unknown.	
My life is insignificant.	
I am a mistake.	
I can lose my salvation.	

Consider recording in your journal any verses you found that speak most specifically to you. Pull them out and post them somewhere you will see them often and can read them out loud. In doing so, you'll be putting on the helmet of salvation.

This incredible list of what your salvation benefits package entails is just one quick sampling from one chapter, from one book of the Bible, from one small corner of God's blessing barn. The fullness of your inheritance speaks to every single area of your mind that the enemy targets with his lies and deceptions. Rehearsing it will renew your mind and cultivate the health you need for making wise choices and living in a way that is pleasing to the Lord.

A NEUROPLASTICIAN AFTER ALL

I have a friend, Dr. Caroline Leaf, who studies neuroplasticity. As a strong believer, she seeks to help God's people understand the effects of toxic thinking on their overall well-being and how submitting their thinking patterns to Christ can create an astounding impact. I'm so grateful for people like her who can break down impossibly difficult concepts into bite-sized pieces that even the most scientifically uninformed among us can understand. (Namely me.) Which is why I was so surprised when she told me that I—a mathematical/scientifically challenged girl—am actually a neuroplastician.

Hang with me for a few minutes and let me explain.

While we tend to consider our thoughts as intangible and theoretical, Dr. Leaf can prove through decades of research that they are actually very real, having measurable effects on our physical brain and bodies. The enemy knows this. He is fully aware of the power of your thoughts in affecting the quality of your entire life. Listen to the doctor's explanation. She says our thoughts "occupy mental 'real estate.' Thoughts are active; they grow and change … Every time you have a thought, it is actively changing your brain and your body—for better or for worse."[5]

By definition neuroplasticity is the brain's ability to reorganize itself by forming new neural connections.

Did you hear that? For better or for worse. You get to determine which side of the spectrum you will swing toward. And here's how:

Turn to 2 Corinthians 10:4-5. Use it to fill in the blanks below.

Since the _____ of our warfare are not of the flesh, but are powerful through God for the demolition of _____. We _____ arguments and every proud thing that is raised up against the knowledge of God, and we _____ _____ _____ _____ to obey Christ (CSB).

If you were considering whether or not to read a novel and words like these were found in the summary on the back cover, what type of book would you expect it to be? What adjectives would you use to describe this book to a friend? Record your thoughts.

Now turn to Romans 12:2 and fill in the blanks.
Do not be conformed to this age, but be _____
by the _____ of your mind, so that you may
_____ what is the good, pleasing, and perfect
will of God (CSB).

These two power-packed passages are *the* battle plan for our defense against the enemy's attempts to infiltrate our minds. They tell us how to transform our thinking and put on the helmet of salvation. I think I can boil it down to three key mission objectives.

STEP #1. IDENTIFY the toxic thought patterns you've been nursing (you've begun that process this week) and recognize them for what they truly are—strongholds that, along with the enemy, you've assisted in constructing within your mind.

In this first step, we hear clear hints of the battle context involved in the fight for our minds. A stronghold in biblical times was a military fortress. Nearly every ancient city had one. It stood at the highest point in their geographical area, built for all to see. It was designed to block and keep out incoming invaders.

What negative thought processes have been elevated to the "highest point" in your mind—over God and His truth in your life?

According to 2 Corinthians 10:4-5, what are strongholds intended to "block and keep out"?

How in particular have you seen this reality to be true in your own experience?

STEP #2. CONFESS errant thought processes to God and agree with Him about your responsibility in helping to construct these strongholds in your life.

Our strongholds are not all the enemy's fault. Every time we've nursed and rehearsed illegitimate thinking, we've added another concrete

> *By definition, a stronghold is a particular belief or attitude (many times incorrect) that you strongly uphold in your life.*

> *The enemy cannot make us do anything. He can only lead us to do things.*[6]
> **Beth Moore**

brick to the construction of a stronghold. Whether those thoughts were in relation to doubt, fear, insecurity, imagination, or something else entirely, rehearsing the enemy's lies made us a partner with the enemy in building up a fortress that has held us captive.

How have you cooperated with the enemy in building your strongholds to their current height and strength? Be specific.

Try to describe your indignation at realizing you've been working with him on some of the same projects.

STEP #3. DISMANTLE the stronghold by taking your thoughts captive, then renewing your perspective and understanding through the concentrated, deliberate application of God's truth.

This is not a passive assignment. It requires you to exercise forethought and be proactive. The same kind of passion and strategy you might put into setting an athletic record or passing a class must define your hands-on approach if you want to destroy a stronghold. Because remember, this is a military fortress we're talking about here, not a flimsy shack. Destroying it requires force and power—the kind that can only come from consistently applying divinely empowered weapons, namely the Word of God.

When Paul instructed us to "take every thought captive" (v. 5), he employed a tone that expresses continuous, ongoing action. So we must understand that being successful at this endeavor will be a lifestyle, not a one-time event. Taking thoughts captive means controlling them instead of allowing them to control you. It means actively replacing the enemy's thinking with God's thinking at every opportunity. When the enemy's lies enter, immediately consider them in light of salvation. Resist the urge to agree with or rehearse the negative thought. Instead replace it—repeatedly, diligently, and verbally—until eventually that brick in our stronghold comes tumbling down.

And it will come down. No matter how long or how difficult this journey has been for you, your vigilance in this area of your life will pay off. Because God Himself will see to it.

In what practical ways would your life be different if these strongholds were torn down and replaced with health and wholeness? How would your loved ones be affected by this change in your mindset?

You'll see the benefits of this commitment in every part of your life, not just your spiritual life. Because neuroscience is catching up with the Bible, discovering (of course) that God has been right all along. According to Dr. Leaf, when we control our thought life, new neural connections and pathways are visibly and measurably formed in the brain—which affects the health and wellness of our physical bodies. In other words, when we "take our thoughts captive," we are quite literally renewing and restoring our minds from a state of unhealthiness and deterioration to a state of wholeness and strength in God. Tapping into our spiritual benefits package not only keeps us from falling prey to the enemy's deception, but also restores previous damage that's been done. When we apply our spiritual inheritance diligently and proactively, we literally change our minds—renewing and rewiring them through God's Word.

That's just how powerful the truth of God really is—living, active, and sharper than a two-edged sword.

> *Finally brothers and sisters, whatever is true, whatever is honorable, whatever is just, whatever is pure, whatever is lovely, whatever is commendable— if there is any moral excellence and if there is any praiseworthy—dwell on these things (Phil. 4:8, CSB).*

Actionable Intel...

DAY 4
MISTAKEN IDENTITY

It was a tragic scene. Abby, a nineteen-year-old college sophomore, was returning home with four other friends on a spring break outing to Disneyland, when the SUV in which she was riding experienced a blowout that turned into a fatal accident. Two of the girls were ejected from the car and died on the scene. Abby was identified as one of them.

As word reached the families back in Arizona—two girls dead, three critically injured—typical parental worry over a college road trip turned to unspeakable grief. Abby's parents spent the next few days combing through the shock and horror, planning the details of their daughter's funeral while three other sets of parents prayed for their own children's recovery, whose bruises and swelling made them hard to recognize as they lay in the hospital.

On Saturday, however, six days after the accident, hospital officials informed two of the families that there had been a horrible mistake. Two of the girls, who bore a striking resemblance, had been misidentified. Parents who'd been sitting by the bedside of a young woman they believed to be their daughter were told the staggering news: She wasn't their daughter after all. Their daughter had actually died in the accident. And Abby's parents? They were given news they could have never imagined receiving: Abby wasn't dead. She was alive.

The initial shock of what they were hearing turned to disbelief. Disbelief then turned to joy. But the joy was mingled, too, with anger—anger that they'd been forced to live for six days in agony because of a reality that wasn't true, a grief they had no need to feel or experience.[7]

It all boiled down to a case of mistaken identity.

The enemy wants you to suffer from a case of mistaken identity, too. Makes his job a whole lot easier. And makes your defenses a lot weaker. He's working overtime to mask your identity in Christ, to keep the truth from coming out—that you are indeed alive and free and empowered by God's own Spirit to fight victoriously against him. The enemy would rather conspire to keep you in a constant state of mourning, grieving over who you wish you were, instead of relishing who you really are. He prefers you insecure and crippled by self-doubt. Lifeless. Comatose.

But his reign of terror is over in our lives. Because now we know the truth. God has "made us alive together with Christ" and has "raised us up with Him and seated us with Him in heavenly places" (Eph. 2:5-6). We will put our helmets on and stand firm against the attacks of the enemy.

IDENTITY REVEALED

David, under the leading of God's Spirit, crafted some beautiful words that unveil the truth of who we really are. Read this passage below:

> O LORD, *You have searched me and known me. You know when I sit down and when I rise up;* You understand my thought from afar. You scrutinize my path and my lying down, and are *intimately acquainted with all my ways.* Even before there is a word on my tongue, behold, O LORD, You know it all. You have enclosed me behind and before, and laid Your hand upon me. Such knowledge is too wonderful for me; it is too high, I cannot attain to it. ...
>
> For *You formed my inward parts; You wove me in my mother's womb.* I will give thanks to You, for *I am fearfully and wonderfully made;* wonderful are Your works, and my soul knows it very well. *My frame was not hidden from You,* when I was made in secret, and skillfully wrought in the depths of the earth; Your eyes have seen my unformed substance; and *in Your book were all written the days that were ordained for me,* when as yet there was not one of them. *How precious also are Your thoughts to me, O God!* How vast is the sum of them! (Ps. 139:1-6,13-17)

Consider each of the highlighted portions of this passage. Choose two that speak most to you and then list them below.

Why do these two statements mean the most to you? Explain in detail.

List any ways these truths contradict what you may have been told by other people throughout your life.

Think of the time and careful attention to detail that God displayed when crafting you inside and out. Consider also the fact that He has searched you fully, knows your deepest thoughts, and still considers you worthwhile, precious, and valuable. These are the kinds of truths your enemy wants to trick you into not believing. So he'll use every opportunity to make you believe it's all a myth—that you are a mistake, horribly flawed, not worthy of love, not capable, not acceptable, or not truly forgiven.

Remember the list of "benefits" from your salvation inheritance package we studied yesterday? Determine which portions of David's psalm correspond with each one.

- I am unworthy.

- I am unloved.

- I am incapable.

- I am undesirable.

- I am unforgivable.

- I am unknown.

- My life is insignificant.

- I am a mistake.

- I can lose my salvation.

IDENTITY IN CHRIST = SALVATION INHERITANCE = THE HELMET OF SALVATION
#ArmorOfGodStudy

From the Old to the New Testament, Scripture emphasizes the value you have as a human being. Better still, as an adopted child in the family of God, you have been recreated by Christ into His masterpiece, prepared for good works to bring Him glory (see Eph. 2:10). The enemy's attacks will always challenge this line of thinking, stirring up insecurities that breed destructive behaviors which are out of alignment with God's will.

Don't miss something very important. Did you notice your salvation benefits package listed in Ephesians 1 is basically a recounting of who you are as a child of God? It's your spiritual identity. This tells you that your identity in Christ is your inheritance. And since we've already established that walking in our inheritance is the helmet of salvation, then wearing it actually means putting on your identity in Christ— renewing your mind according to it, then adapting your behavior to align with it. So look at this equation:

Identity in Christ = Salvation Inheritance = The Helmet of Salvation

What does this equation reveal about why the enemy attacks your sense of identity—who you are in Christ?

YOUR IDENTITY IS YOUR WEAPONRY.
#ArmorofGodStudy

Now, think back all the way to the beginning of this study when you wrote the circumstance or person that is most difficult in your life right now. Remember? In the oval on page 13. (It's been six weeks, so feel free to update or change this if you need to.)

What are the lies that the enemy has used in this circumstance to attack your mind?

How could solid footing in your spiritual identity help to defray his attempts and ultimately your reactions and responses to this circumstance/person?

Your identity is your weaponry. Putting on the helmet of your salvation is akin to knowing who you are in Christ, fortifying your thinking with it, and living in a way that is congruent with it. When you do this, you break the enemy's stronghold and also tap into the power to deflect future attacks.

THIS MEANS WAR

Renewing our minds and deflecting the enemy's advances to control them is not for the faint of heart. It requires vigilance. Aggressive, proactive attention.

I know one woman who has taken the concept of wearing her helmet very seriously. She is an extremely busy homeschool mom of five kids. She also helps run the women's ministry at our local church. I don't know if I've ever met a woman whose schedule is more packed than hers. Which is why I was intrigued one day when I got in her car and noticed a small clip attached to her dashboard. Tucked inside it was a 3 x 5 card on which she'd written a Scripture verse. Just one.

When I commented on it, she explained to me that since she spent so much time running errands and getting kids from one place to the next, she'd decided to keep one verse on her dashboard for seven days. That way, all day long, whenever her eyes happened to land on it, she'd be reminded of its truth and encouraged to implement it in her life.

But wait, it gets better. Because by the end of that week, she was able to share with me how she'd not only memorized the verse, but could also relate several instances where that verse had "come to life" for her—informing her decisions, renewing her mind, changing her perspective, redirecting her responses and actions, allowing her to hear God's guidance for specific situations that unfolded during the week. She explained that when thoughts contrary to the truth in that verse would seek to infiltrate her mind, she'd zero in on that 3 x 5 card and quote it out loud. She didn't use her busy schedule as an excuse for being lax in

> *Set your mind on the things above, not on the things that are on earth. For you have died and your life is hidden with Christ in God (Col. 3:2-3).*

putting on her helmet. She wanted to ensure that she was on guard and prepared for the enemy's attempts to target her.

When you are in a war, you don't relax your resolve or disengage from active warfare. You don't take a vacation. You do whatever you need to do to keep that helmet on and in position throughout your day, every day. You "talk of them when you sit in your house and when you walk by the way and when you lie down and when you rise up. You shall bind them as a sign on your hand and they shall be as frontals on your forehead. You shall write them on the doorposts of your house and on your gates" (Deut. 6:7-9). Or even on the dashboard of your car.

Where are some strategic places you could post truth tomorrow so you'll have it on hand throughout the day? Maybe in some of the same places you've been posting your prayers?

Maybe a good place to start is with the Identity in Christ (pp.182-183) that I've given you. Photocopy it, tear it out of this workbook, do whatever you need to do to position it front and center in your life. It is a biblical treasure of mind-renewing, stronghold-imploding, life-transforming insight. Read it and reread it until you feel it taking root and acting as a helmet of protection over your mind.

There's a war raging. Make no mistake. And never fall for mistaken identity.

Actionable Intel...

Be sober-minded, be alert! Your adversary the devil is prowling around like a roaring lion, looking for anyone he can devour (1 Pet. 5:8, CSB).

DAY 5
STRATEGY SESSION

I've got something personal to share with you today before you begin crafting your prayer strategy. But first, answer this question:

If you've uncovered negative thought patterns in your life this week, can you pinpoint a specific event or situation in your life that may have given the enemy ample opportunity to perpetuate them? If you feel comfortable, prepare to share this with someone in your group or someone whom you trust.

I had a difficult time in high school. But from the outside looking in, you would never have known it. My grades were fairly decent, and I was very active—I rarely let others see my true feelings (which probably made the struggle even worse). But by and large, I was only accepted by a very small core group of friends—for whom I am eternally grateful. Two other major groups, however, with which I had connections through sports and my interests, never truly accepted me as their own. When I would try to meld into one group, they brushed me aside. Then when I tried to escape to the other, they did they same. Feelings of rejection settled deep into my soul.

Have you ever been *(Circle any that apply)*:
- belittled by peers?
- ignored by a parent?
- betrayed by a friend?
- bullied?
- laughed at by the cool crowd?
- abused at the hand of someone you trusted?
- hurt by an authority figure?
- crippled by grief over the loss of a loved one?
- rejected by someone you thought you loved?
- something else similarly upsetting?

The enemy will attach his lies to the coattails of those negative experiences and send them right into the center of your mind. Once you are hurt by something someone does or says to you—even if it is unintentional or a natural part of life—the enemy will take advantage of the opportunity and begin weaving lies about who you are and your hope in Christ, using that specific event as a case in point.

In my case, for example, the enemy made me believe I was unaccepted by certain groups of my peers for one reason: I was unacceptable. Oh, boy, the enemy had a field day with that one throughout the remainder of my high school and college years, making me constantly feel the need to prove my value in hopes that others would accept me into their company. It's an exhausting way to live. It wasn't until my early twenties that I even noticed this pattern and could clearly see why I was behaving this way.

Since then, I've had to determine daily to be vigilant and go to war for my mind by rehearsing my spiritual inheritance every chance I get. And because I'm aware of this stronghold, I've particularly challenged myself not to say or do anything that originates from a place of insecurity. So, for example, before I choose to accept an invitation to that person's party, or respond to that tweet, or join this organization, or add a comment to a conversation, I stop and make myself consider the motivation behind it: Am I doing this because I want the approval of a person or group of people? Or am I doing this from a posture of value and worth in Christ? I want to train and discipline myself not to placate old feelings that the enemy is dredging up from my past. This exercise has made it startlingly clear how many things I say or do primarily to oblige my insecurities instead of resting in my value as a child of God.

Why don't you try this challenge and see what you discover?

For the next seven days, try not to say or do anything in response to feelings of insecurity, fear, or really anything that is out of alignment with your true identity in Christ. You might be surprised at how quiet you become.

But today, gather up your Actionable Intel and craft a prayer strategy that will let the enemy know you mean business. Be as specific and honest as you can. Let your prayer resound with the promises of God over your life. Then post it and pray it out loud as often as you can.

The enemy won't stand a chance against you!

"OUR PRAYING NEEDS TO BE PRESSED AND PURSUED WITH AN ENERGY THAT NEVER TIRES, A PERSISTENCY WHICH WILL NOT BE DENIED, AND A COURAGE THAT NEVER FAILS."

E.M. BOUNDS

MY INHERITANCE AND IDENTITY IN CHRIST

The benefits and blessings bestowed upon us as redeemed children of God are more numerous than we can count. But the following list, taken directly from Scripture, is surely an impressive sampling. I don't recall where I came across this particular list or who gave it to me. It's been in my study notes for years. I just know I love it, and I share it with you, hoping it will give you great confidence and encouragement in Christ.

- I am a child of God (John 1:12).

- I have peace with God (Rom. 5:1).

- The Holy Spirit lives in me (1 Cor. 3:16).

- I have access to God's wisdom (Jas. 1:5).

- I am helped by God (Heb. 4:16).

- I am reconciled to God (Rom. 5:11).

- I am not condemned by God (Rom. 8:1).

- I am justified (Rom. 5:1).

- I have Christ's righteousness (Rom. 5:19; 2 Cor. 5:21).

- I am Christ's ambassador (2 Cor. 5:20).

- I am completely forgiven (Col. 1:14).

- I am tenderly loved by God (Jer. 31:3).

- I am the sweet fragrance of Christ to God (2 Cor. 2:15).

- I am a temple in which God dwells (1 Cor. 3:16).

- I am blameless and beyond reproach (Col. 1:22).

- I am the salt of the earth (Matt. 5:13).

- I am the light of the world (Matt. 5:14).

- I am a branch on Christ's vine (John 15:1,5).

- I am Christ's friend (John 15:5).

- I am chosen by Christ to bear fruit (John 15:6).

- I am a joint heir with Christ, sharing his inheritance with him (Rom. 8:17).

- I am united to the Lord, one spirit with him (1 Cor. 6:17).

- I am a member of Christ's body (1 Cor. 12:27).

- I am a saint (Eph. 1:1).

- I am hidden with Christ in God (Col. 3:3).

- I am chosen by God, holy and dearly loved (Col. 3:12).

- I am a child of the light (1 Thess. 5:5).

- I am holy, and I share in God's heavenly calling (Heb. 3:1).

- I am sanctified (Heb. 2:11).

- I am one of God's living stones, being built up in Christ as a spiritual house (1 Pet. 2:5).

- I am a member of a chosen race, a royal priesthood, a holy nation, a people for God's own possession and created to sing his praises (1 Pet. 2:9-10).

- I am firmly rooted and built up in Christ (Col. 2:7).

- I am born of God, and the evil one cannot touch me (1 John 5:18).

- I have the mind of Christ (1 Cor. 2:16).

- I may approach God with boldness, freedom, and confidence (Eph. 3:12).

- I have been rescued from Satan's domain and transferred into the kingdom of Christ (Col. 1:13).

- I have been made complete in Christ (Col. 2:10).

- I have been given a spirit of power, love, and self-discipline (2 Tim. 1:7).

- I have been given great and precious promises by God (2 Pet. 1:4).

- My needs are met by God (Phil. 4:19).

- I am a prince (princess) in God's kingdom (John 1:12; 1 Tim. 6:15).

- I have been bought with a price, and I belong to God (1 Cor. 6:19,20).

- I have been adopted as God's child (Eph. 1:5).

- I have direct access to God through the Holy Spirit (Eph. 2:18).

- I am assured that all things are working together for good (Rom. 8:28).

- I am free from any condemning charges against me (Rom. 8:31).

- I cannot be separated from the love of God (Rom. 8:35).

- I have been established, anointed, and sealed by God (2 Cor. 1:21,22).

- I am confident that the good work that God has begun in me will be perfected (Phil. 1:6).

- I am a citizen of heaven (Phil. 3:20).

- I am a personal witness of Christ's (Acts 1:8).

- I am God's coworker (2 Cor. 6:1; 1 Cor. 3:9).

- I am seated with Christ in the heavenly realm (Eph. 2:6).

- I am God's workmanship (Eph. 2:10).

- I can do all things through Christ, who gives me the strength I need (Phil. 4:13).

THE SWORD OF THE SPIRIT

Think about your childhood arguments with your siblings or friends. When you felt attacked, were there certain comebacks you relied on to defend yourself or somehow fight back against your so-called enemy? Share a few with the group.

We often use words as weapons, like biting comebacks meant to deflect or cold remarks designed to hurt and create distance. God has given us a powerful weapon to fight back against our enemy's schemes, and it's more than just words.

Read Ephesians 6:10-19 one final time in your Bible. Pay close attention to the final piece of armor described in verse 17. What is it? Write the answer below.

The sword of the Spirit is unique for a couple of reasons. The first reason is that it's the only piece of armor that Paul actually described in Ephesians 6. For most of the pieces of armor, Paul was simply reminding his readers of truths he had explained in-depth earlier in his letter. But the sword of the Spirit? He wanted to make sure to further clarify beyond any reasonable doubt exactly what the sword of the Spirit is: the Word of God. Scripture. In other words, the Sword of the Spirit is the very truths you've been studying for these past six weeks.

Look at the list of weapons in Ephesians 6:16-17: the shield, the helmet, and the sword. Notice that the sword is the only offensive weapon. The shield and the helmet were meant to protect against attack, but a soldier would use a sword to fight. To tear down the strongholds in your life, take back spiritual ground, and walk in continued victory, you must be proactive and on the offensive. Paul is telling us that when it comes to standing firm against the enemy, we shouldn't always be on the defense. Often, we have to take a posture.

Roman soldiers typically carried two kinds of swords. One was the large broadsword we discussed last week. It often took two hands to wield a broadsword, and they were three to four feet in length. The other sword, the one Paul was calling to mind in Ephesians 6:17, was smaller, double-edged, and more dagger-like. It was perfect for hand-to-hand combat. This was the sword you used when an enemy was right in your face.

Sometimes it feels like Satan is right in our faces, when we're riddled with fear or overcome by insecurity or temptation. How have you witnessed the enemy's personal attacks in your own life or that of someone you love?

That's why God has given us this final weapon, which is His very Word.

Three different words in the original Scripture are translated *Word of God*. Look at each of them below and discuss the differences with your group.

1. *Graphe* **– refers literally to the actual ink on the page. It's the words, paper, and binding that actually make up the book itself.**

2. *Logos* **– refers to the meaning of the Bible. It's the explanation, understanding, and application of the graphe by the hearer (Heb. 4:12).**

3. *Rhema* **– refers to the Word of God as it is illuminated by the Holy Spirit so that it speaks to us individually and personally giving us individual direction, guidance, and confirmation (John 6:63).**

The Word of God is the *rhema* of God, the spoken Word of God to you and to your life. The rhema is when you're sitting in church, and the pastor begins to preach, and you feel like you are the only person in the room because the verse he is talking about is personal to you. That's God speaking to you. It's when you're having your personal quiet time, and you come across a verse in the Bible, and it's like the Holy Spirit took out a divine highlighter. The verse leaps off the page and grips your soul. You know God is convicting, challenging, and speaking to you. That's the rhema.

The rhema is the power of God. This is why I've asked you to record Actionable Intel throughout this study. Those truths God has called to your attention as you've studied His Word, the promises that you carefully crafted into strategic prayers against the enemy? That's the rhema, the sword of the Spirit, the power of God.

As strategic as our enemy has been against us, we ought to be more strategic in our prayers against him. So, don't stop now. Keep studying His Word and gathering Actionable Intel against him. Make it a lifetime endeavor. Keep a record of the Scripture the Spirit hands you so you can stand firm against the enemy and his attacks. You are fighting a daily battle against a real enemy, but you can live in victory.

LEADER GUIDE

SIZING UP THE ENEMY

A vital part of this study will include journaling and prayer. Encourage students to use a blank journal or notebook to record their Actionable Intel and prayers, as well as the perforated prayer cards in the back of the book.

FOR STARTERS: Kick off the conversation by asking students the discussion questions that open Week 1's group discussion on page 8. Discuss the story about Priscilla's cousin.

READ EPHESIANS 6:10-12 and talk about the armor of God. Stress that warriors wear armor when they are going into battle. As believers, we face an invisible enemy we war against every day.

TALK IT OUT and work through the remainder of the discussion guide. Help participants to fill in the blanks of the five key points: 1. The battle is <u>unavoidable</u>; 2. The enemy is <u>invisible</u>; 3. The location is <u>accessible</u>; 4. Your weapons are not <u>physical</u>; and, 5. The victory is <u>irrevocable</u>. Use these questions to spur further discussion:

- How is this teaching similar or different from what you've heard about the enemy in the past?

- What truth jumped out as you reflect on what you've learned today?

CLOSE by emphasizing the importance of writing prayer strategies throughout this study. Refer to page 192 and go over the prayer strategies to help those who may be unsure of how to proceed. Close in prayer, asking God to help you and your students to stand in the victory God has already won for us through Jesus.

SESSION 2
THE BELT OF TRUTH

FOR STARTERS: Review what students learned as they studied "Sizing Up The Enemy" in Week 1. Encourage them to share highlights from their Actionable Intel and their most important insights from each day. Turn the conversation to this week's topic by asking the discussion questions on page 38:

- What's your tendency? Do you personally overestimate or underestimate the enemy's influence in the circumstances of your life? What effect does this inclination have in your life? (See page 18 of your homework.)

READ EPHESIANS 6:13-14 and invite students with different translations to read them aloud. Point out that our enemy always takes a personalized, targeted approach in his schemes against us, which makes it imperative that we base our lives, thoughts, and decisions on the truth God has revealed to us.

TALK IT OUT by working through the rest of the discussion guide that begins on page 38. Guide students to fill in the blanks about the belt of truth, stressing that it allows us to <u>stand firm</u> against the schemes of the devil, and it makes us truly <u>free</u> to experience the abundant life we were created for. Spark further discussion with these questions:

- How might your life be different if you strengthen your spiritual core?

• What will it take to make the commitment to spiritual strength training for your core?

CLOSE by referencing Numbers 13:1-33, recapping the story as needed. Discuss how trusting God's Word would have changed the outcome. Close in prayer, asking the Holy Spirit to help us submit our feelings, lives, and futures to God, trusting Him.

SESSION 3
THE BREASTPLATE OF RIGHTEOUSNESS

FOR STARTERS: Encourage students to share a few truths that stuck out to them this week. Talk about how the belt of truth is a "hanger" for all the other pieces of armor and why that's important. Introduce the breastplate of righteousness with the discussion questions on page 66.

READ EPHESIANS 6:14 and talk about how the breastplate is a piece of armor designed to protect. Stress that unrighteousness in our lives creates a weak place where Satan can gain a foothold.

TALK IT OUT using the discussion guide. Share a few examples of moments when you are personally more susceptible to temptation (p. 68). Invite volunteers to share a few examples from their lives. Use the questions below to invite more conversation:

• Like the breastplate on the armor protects the physical body, how does the spiritual piece of armor, the breastplate of righteousness, protect the believer?

• Can we meet God's standard of righteousness on our own? Why or why not? How has Jesus solved this problem for us?

• Why is it important to recognize that it is the Holy Spirit who sanctifies us rather than trying to do it in our own power?

CLOSE by encouraging your students to be intentional about crafting their prayer strategies. Explain that this activates their spiritual armor. Make yourself available to those who may have questions.

SESSION 4
THE SHOES OF PEACE

FOR STARTERS: Share with your group something new you learned or were challenged by during this week's homework. Review the activity and Scripture passages on page 85 related to putting on specific virtues and their spiritual benefits. Invite students to share about the verses that most encouraged them personally. Turn the conversation to the shoes of peace by asking the discussion questions on page 94.

READ EPHESIANS 6:14-15 emphasizing the shoes of peace that make your feet ready and prepared. Explain that Satan wants to use the storms in our lives to break us, to rob us of God's victory and peace, but it doesn't have to be that way.

TALK IT OUT using the remainder of the discussion guide to direct the conversation. Help students ponder what God's peace can do in our lives by filling in the blanks on page 95: gives us a firm <u>grip</u> in a world that is not <u>firm</u>; gives us <u>stability</u>; allows us to keep our footing; and keeps us sane. The following questions may help guide further discussion:

- Why do you think Paul attached shoes to the characteristic of peace?

- How have you experienced the peace of God in your life and how do you explain it to someone?

- How is God's peace different from the world's idea of peace? Explain.

CLOSE by explaining that we cannot experience the peace of God if we are not in a relationship with Him through Jesus. Clearly present the gospel for those who may have never placed their faith in Jesus. Close in a time of personal prayer, inviting students to consider Christ's invitation. Pray that students would experience the thankfulness and guidance His peace brings.

SESSION 5
THE SHIELD OF FAITH

FOR STARTERS: Call for students to share something they learned during this week's study. Ask:

- What are some areas of your life where you need to be on the offensive instead of the defensive, taking back ground from the enemy?

- What would this process look like in a practical sense? (See your answers from your homework on page 118.)

Introduce today's topic by asking the discussion questions at the top of page 124.

READ EPHESIANS 6:16 and remind students of the enemy's attacks upon our faith and how we need to be prepared to defend ourselves.

TALK IT OUT using the rest of the discussion guide to shape the conversation. Guide students to fill in the blanks on page 125 about active faith: 1. Faith reveals a reliance on God; 2. Faith is what you say you believe in action; 3. Faith is when you act like God is telling you the truth. Note the specifics about faith in the teaching.

- How is the truth of our faith reflected in our actions and attitudes?

- What have been the greatest challenges to your faith? When have you seemed to be strongest in your faith?

- When have you seen someone come to The Faith Place and step out in active faith? What did you learn from that situation?

CLOSE by encouraging students to stay faithful in writing down their prayer strategies in their journals or notebooks. End the session by praying for the courage to put your faith into action this week, asking God to conquer the fear and extinguish the distractions in your lives.

SESSION 6
THE HELMET OF SALVATION

FOR STARTERS: Review Ephesians 6:16 and your answers to the question on page 135. Why do you think Paul may have gone to greater lengths to accentuate the benefits of the shield of faith?

Call attention to the turtle formation on page 137. What does this teach us about how we should concern ourselves with building up the faith of others? How should active faith strengthen the broader community of Christ?

Focus students' attention on the helmet of salvation by asking students to discuss the concept of identity. Use the discussion question on page 152.

READ EPHESIANS 6:10-19 to review the armor of God we are to put on. Review the three pieces of armor we're to put on and the three pieces we're called to pick up. Explain that salvation is not just about saving us from hell, but also equipping us to live victoriously.

TALK IT OUT using the remainder of the discussion guide to shape the conversation. Call for a student to read aloud Romans 12:1-2. As a group, discuss what these verses have to do with the helmet of salvation. Share examples of how God's Word has renewed your mind and changed toxic thought patterns or beliefs. Invite students to share, too. Other questions include:

- What is Jesus currently doing in your life and how does your relationship with Him impact you daily?

- What are some ways to describe the truth of salvation and the helmet of salvation with others?

CLOSE the session by working together to create a list of verses from Scripture that fight back against common strongholds or toxic thoughts your students face. Close in prayer.

THE SWORD OF THE SPIRIT

FOR STARTERS: Invite students to share something new they learned or discovered through this week's study. As a group, talk about what applying salvation to our daily lives actually looks like. Start the discussion of this week's topic by asking the question at the top of page 185.

READ EPHESIANS 6:10-20 and challenge students to think of this group session as the start of a new study as they consider the sword of the Spirit. Explain that they don't need a week of homework on the sword of the Spirit because they've been doing it throughout this entire study as they've dug into God's Word and applied it to their lives in their Actionable Intel.

TALK IT OUT using the rest of the discussion plan to guide the discussion. Challenge students to consider the next steps they will take:

- How will you continue your prayer strategies and spend time in God's Word?

- Review "My Inheritance and Identity in Christ" (pp. 182-183) and discuss how the truth of God's Word has changed you and is still changing you.

- Encourage students to continue to write down prayer strategies as a habit even after this study is over.

CLOSE in prayer, thanking God for how He has worked in your life and those of your students throughout this study.

ENDNOTES

SESSION 1

1. James E. Rosscup, "The Importance of Prayer in Ephesians," *The Master's Seminary Journal,* Volume 6, Number 1 (Spring 1995), 58.
2. Clinton E. Arnold, *Ephesians: Power and Magic* (New York, NY: Cambridge University Press, 1989), 14-15.
3. Chip Ingram, *The Invisible War: What Every Believer Needs to Know* (Grand Rapids, MI: Baker Books, 2006), 28.

SESSION 2

1. I. H. Marshall, A. R. Millard, J. I. Packer, & D. J. Wiseman, eds., *New Bible Dictionary.* 3rd ed. Downers Grove, IL: InterVarsity Press, 1996, 682.
2. G. R. Watson, *The Roman Soldier* (Ithaca, NY: Cornell University Press, 1969), 63.
3. Pat Southern, *The Roman Army* (Santa Barbara, CA: ABC-CLIO, Inc., 2006), 154.
4. D. G. Reid, R. D. Linder, B. L. Shelley, and H. S. Stout, *Dictionary of Christianity in America.* Downers Grove, IL: InterVarsity Press.
5. Charles Spurgeon, as quoted by *TruthSource* (online), cited 12 June 2015. Available on the Internet: *truthsource.com.*
6. Pat Southern, 154.

SESSION 3

1. Larry Richards, *The Full Armor of God* (Minneapolis, MN: Chosen Books, 2013), 98.
2. Pat Southern, 156.
3. John R. W. Stott, *The Message of Ephesians* (Downers Grove, IL: InterVarsity Press: 1979), 279.
4. Peter O'Brien, *The Letter to the Ephesians* (Grand Rapids, MI: Wm. B. Eerdman's Publishing Co., 1999), 327.
5. Tony Evans, *Victory in Spiritual Warfare* (Eugene, OR: Harvest House Publishers, 2011), 75.

SESSION 4

1. Larry Richards, *The Full Armor of God* (Minneapolis, MN: Chosen Books, 2013), 79.
2. M. C. Bishop and J. C. Coulston, *Roman Military Equipment from the Punic Wars to the Fall of Rome*, 2nd ed. (Oxford, UK: Oxbow Books, 2006), 112-113.
3. Ibid., 112.
4. Charles Spurgeon, *Spiritual Warfare in a Believer's Life* (Lynnwood, WA: Emerald Books, 1993), 139.
5. Peter O'Brien, 475.
6. Pat Southern, 155.
7. Thomas R. Yoder Neufeld, "Put on the Armour of God," *The Divine Warrior from Isaiah to Ephesians* (Sheffeld, UK: Sheffeld Academic Press, Ltd., 1997), 29.

SESSION 5

1. M.C. Bishop and J.C. Coulston, 100.
2. A. W. Tozer, *The Knowledge of the Holy* (New York, NY: Harper Collins, 1961), 62.
3. Jon Paramenter, "Warfare, Indian," *Dictionary of American History* (online), cited 18 May 2015. Available on the Internet: *encyclopedia.com.*
4. Chip Ingram, 124.

SESSION 6

1. Douglas Mangum, Rachel Klippenstein, Derek R. Brown, Rebekah Hurst, *Lexham Theological Dictionary* (Lexham Press, 2014).
2. M.C. Bishop and J.C. Coulston, 7.
3. Ibid., 101.
4. R. Kent Hughes, *Ephesians* (Wheaton, IL: Crossway Books, 1990), 241.
5. Dr. Caroline Leaf, Who Switched Off My Brain? (Nashville, TN: Thomas Nelson Publishers, 1982), 13-14.
6. Beth Moore, *Breaking Free* (Nashville, TN: B&H Publishers, 2000), 230.
7. "Mourning the Wrong Girl," CBS News (online), cited 12 June 2015. Available on the Internet: *http://www.cbsnews.com/news/mourning-the-wrong-girl/*
Quote on page 181: E. M. Bounds, as quoted by *Good Reads* (online), cited 12 June 2015. Available on the Internet: *goodreads.com.*

PRAYER STRATEGIES

Below you'll find some broad guidelines and framework for your prayer strategies. As you craft your prayers, be authentic, personal, and intentional. You can always come to this page for inspiration and help as you seek to remain anchored and strong in your writing.

My hope is that you'll not only emerge from this Bible study with six strategies locked in place but also a habit for intentional prayer that reverberates throughout the rest of your life.

P—PRAISE: Gratitude to God for who He is and what He's already done should thread throughout every prayer, because ultimately His name and His fame are the only reasons any of this matters.

R—REPENTANCE: Expect prayer to expose where you're still resisting Him—not only resisting His commands, but resisting the manifold blessings and benefits He gives to those who follow. Line your strategies with repentance: the courage to trust, and turn, and walk His way.

A—ASKING: Make your requests known. Be personal and specific. Write down details of your own issues and difficulties as they relate to the broader issue we discussed in that week of study, as well as how you perhaps see the enemy's hand at work in them or where you suspect he might be aiming next.

Y—YES: "All of God's promises," the Bible says, "have been fulfilled in Christ with a resounding 'Yes!'" (2 Cor. 1:20, NLT). You may not understand everything that is happening in your life right now, but any possible explanation pales in comparison to what you do know because of your faith in God's goodness and assurances. So allow your prayer to be accentuated with His own words from Scripture, His promises to you that correspond to your need. There is nothing more powerful than praying God's own Word. Because even at the mention of His name, the enemy buckles in certain defeat.

Get the most from your study.

Customize your Bible study time with a guided experience and additional resources.

The Bible study you are holding in your hands is more than just a biblical description of the believer's inventory. It is an action plan for putting on your armor and developing a personalized strategy to secure victory against the enemy. Join Priscilla Shirer on a 7-week journey as you learn of the invisible war that rages all around you.

- Learn to be strong in the Lord and in the strength of His might (Eph. 6:10).

- Discover what to wear to ensure victory and employ the secret weapon to stop the devil in his tracks.

- Develop a personalized strategy to promptly put the enemy in his place.

- Take advantage of your position in Christ and experience the tangible, long-term effects of victory in practical, everyday living.

Lifeway designs trustworthy experiences that fuel ministry. Today, the ministries of Lifeway reach more than 160 countries around the globe. For specific information on Lifeway Students, visit lifeway.com/students.

ADDITIONAL
RESOURCES

THE ARMOR OF GOD BIBLE STUDY BOOK FOR WOMEN
A 7-week Bible study for women

UNSEEN: THE ARMOR OF GOD FOR KIDS ACTIVITY BOOK
A 7-week Bible study for older kids

DEFINED BIBLE STUDY FOR TEEN GIRLS
An 8-week Bible study on our identity by Priscilla Shirer

DEFINED BIBLE STUDY FOR TEEN GUYS
An 8-week Bible study on our identity by Stephen and Alex Kendrick

MY PRAYER STRATEGY

_____

_____

_____

_____

_____

_____

_____

_____

_____

_____

_____

_____

_____

_____

_____

MY PRAYER STRATEGY

_____

_____

_____

_____

_____

_____

_____

_____

_____

_____

_____

_____

_____

_____

MY PRAYER STRATEGY

MY PRAYER STRATEGY

MY PRAYER STRATEGY

_____
_____
_____
_____
_____
_____
_____
_____
_____
_____
_____
_____
_____
_____

MY PRAYER STRATEGY

_____
_____
_____
_____
_____
_____
_____
_____
_____
_____
_____
_____
_____
_____

MY PRAYER STRATEGY

MY PRAYER STRATEGY

MY PRAYER STRATEGY

MY PRAYER STRATEGY

MY PRAYER STRATEGY

_____

_____

_____

_____

_____

_____

_____

_____

_____

_____

_____

_____

MY PRAYER STRATEGY

_____

_____

_____

_____

_____

_____

_____

_____

_____

_____

_____

_____

MY  PRAYER STRATEGY

MY PRAYER STRATEGY